LESSONS FROM A GOOD DEATH

Lessons from a Good Death

DR EMMA GOODALL

Healthy Possibilities Pty Ltd

CONTENTS

DEDICATION
xi

~ 1 ~
Death and Grief
1

~ 2 ~
Revenge
3

~ 3 ~
Managing Life's Challenges
4

~ 4 ~
Sorry
7

~ 5 ~
Feeling in the Moment
9

~ 6 ~

A Helping Hand

12

~ 7 ~

Reaching Out

14

~ 8 ~

Late

17

~ 9 ~

Reconciliation

19

~ 10 ~

Driving

22

~ 11 ~

Perceptions

24

~ 12 ~

Perception

27

~ 13 ~

Sadness

30

~ 14 ~

Tired

32

~ 15 ~
Stuck
34

~ 16 ~
Don't Get Stuck
37

~ 17 ~
Laughter (or lack of)
39

~ 18 ~
Mould on Cheese
42

~ 19 ~
Blossom
44

~ 20 ~
Connection
47

~ 21 ~
Broken Record/Perseveration
49

~ 22 ~
Technology
52

~ 23 ~
One for Sorrow, Two for Joy
54

~ 24 ~

Loss

57

~ 25 ~

Lonely Versus Alone

59

~ 26 ~

Lonely When Alone

62

~ 27 ~

A Lifetime Ago

64

~ 28 ~

Kia Kaha (Stay Strong)

66

~ 29 ~

Exhaustion

69

~ 30 ~

Pain is Exhausting

72

~ 31 ~

Anxiety

74

~ 32 ~

Anxious

77

~ 33 ~
Boxes & Filing Cabinets
79

~ 34 ~
Love
81

~ 35 ~
Love & Kindness
83

~ 36 ~
Using Humour to be Kind
86

~ 37 ~
Windows & Doors
88

~ 38 ~
Time
92

~ 39 ~
Friends
94

~ 40 ~
People
97

~ 41 ~
Kindness & Joy
99

~ 42 ~
Struggles
101

~ 43 ~
Folded Rocks
103

~ 44 ~
Secrets
104

~ 45 ~
Milestones
106

~ 46 ~
The End
110

~ 47 ~
Ideas From Jane
113

~ 48 ~
Things to do to Prepare
114

~ 49 ~
The Inspiration & the Author
115

ABOUT THE AUTHOR

116

To everyone who has been a part of both my journey and Jane's.
Thanks

Copyright © 2020 by Dr Emma Goodall

All rights reserved. No part of this book may be reproduced in any manner whatsoever without written permission except in the case of brief quotations embodied in critical articles and reviews.

First Printing, 2020

~ 1 ~

DEATH AND GRIEF

by Dr Emma Goodall

'Our relationship in Oamaru Stone'
E.Goodall (2020) photograph only

Grief is an individual journey, even though the grief may be shared widely, it is in many ways held closely too. For some people, open and outwardly expressed grief forms part of a communal mourning, whilst for others there is a silence punctuated by awkward but well-meaning comments. The loss of a loved one to death is both emotionally and physically painful. I did not know how physically painful this type of grief was until my head was pounding and my neck almost choked in pain.

A good death for the person who died, is not necessarily good for those left behind and vice versa. When my wife, Jane, died, she died the good death that she had always wanted. Her death was instant, painless and she was at home. It was also sudden and in many ways completely unexpected and in others totally predictable. I am a Buddhist, but this is not a religious book.

This book is both a tribute to Jane's kindness and compassion for others in life and a record of my grief. What was helpful and what was not. It is full of hope and despair, much like life. I do not believe that any of our grief journeys are the same, but in understanding what others have experienced it can be helpful. The sections subtitled Emma are from my grief journey blog posts. I have blogged for many years in one form or another, to manage grief associated with observing the trauma, suicidal ideation and death of loved ones, whether friends, family or students that I was teaching.

Alternate chapters with, inspired by Dr Jane, are stories taken from her life, either shared with me or told to me by Jane before she died.

~ 2 ~

REVENGE

"The best form of revenge is success. People said I couldn't be a Doctor. I became a Doctor."

Dr Jane (repeatedly)

Dr Jane Nugent's mobile clinic during COVID-19 lockdown
E.Goodall (2020)

~ 3 ~

MANAGING LIFE'S CHALLENGES

Waves crashing into rocks. Australia
E.Goodall (2018)

For many people around the world, the current COVID-19 pandemic has brought to the forefront challenges in a range of life areas. For me, the life challenge that I am managing is the death of my wife during the pandemic. Even though she did not die of, nor even with COVID-19, the pandemic has impacted everything around her death, and therefore how I can manage this life challenge.

One of the things I have chosen to do, in order to manage this life challenge in a way that is most positive and helpful for me, is to share the journey. As an autistic adult, I am not always comfortable sharing my journey. However, in losing my wife, I lost not just my partner in life and business, but also my best friend and my interpreter for the wider world, my sounding board and the person who pushed me and inspired me to life a live of compassion and kindness even when challenged. Jane, often known as Dr Jane, or Dr Nugent, was a GP with the biggest heart, a beautiful smile, and the most compassionate and kindest person I had ever met. She was determined to make the world a better place, and to help everyone and every dog that she possibly could. Her death impacted so many, and the outpouring of aroha (love) and grief was overwhelming, but also comforting. I chose to take comfort in that shared loss and shared grief. I accepted all offers of help (even when emotionally unable to answer the phone, I would text or msg people and was so grateful for all the practical support and meals that appeared).

The other important thing I chose to do, was to celebrate Jane's life and the time that we had been together (14 years) rather than focusing on what I lost, I want to try and focus on what I have gained over this time. Which is a lot, in no particular order; a son, a whanau, extended family, new friends, a sense of place and purpose that I could see was hugely valued which further increased confidence and competence, a PhD journey that was less difficult than many people's, a sense of family and home that did not encompass loneliness.

Obviously, (or maybe not), this life challenge is hard to manage. I have discovered that grief can be so intense that it manifests as physical pain, and nausea. I have discovered that quiet moments of connection to my love for Jane and her wairua (spirit) can briefly heal my heart and warm my soul. I have discovered that many many people really to want to connect, to provide support and kindness. I have discovered that sayings that I have used to manage life challenges over the years do indeed have a purpose and a place, though they are not necessarily 100% applicable.

For example, I deeply believe and have been saying for the last 20 years; *'everything changes, nothing is permanent'* and *'there is no point in getting upset or distressed about things that you can't do anything about'*.

The COVID-19 pandemic, and the requirement to stay at home/lockdown, have worked beautifully to manage the challenge of shifting from lots of travel and work interactions to being home 24/7 and only zoom and Jane for company. Jane worked more in the period from the start of the pandemic than I was comfortable with, but it made her really happy. She could provide health services to people who were scared and needed them, in ways that brought them both physical and emotional relief and comfort and educated them at the same time. This was her career high point, where she was living her core values.

But for her death, these sayings were less helpful. She died instantly and painlessly, and then everything changed. I was shown very clearly that nothing is permanent. But it was jarring and heartbreaking, even though there was nothing I could do to bring her back, and I did try, I tried very hard but to no avail. In the end what helps manage this life challenge of heartbreak, is what has always helped me manage life. I help others. I keep moving forward one step at a time, with the same life purpose and values; to help alleviate suffering and to act with kindness and compassion. I am learning to be comfortable with the uncomfortable, to realise it is ok to be sad, because feelings of sadness and grief will not be forever, because nothing is permanent and everything changes.

Arohanui Jane – kia kaha to everyone.

~ 4 ~

SORRY

Inspired by Dr Jane

Our Wedding Rings
2020

"You need to apologize when you do something wrong, make the wrong decision. Even to a child, especially to our son."

Jane was big on apologies, she was big on telling the truth, even if it was not what someone wanted to hear. She taught me to re-think the old adage that 'children should be seen and not heard' with her story about how she had to cut a Thomas the Tank Engine toy out of our son's hair when he was young. Twenty years later she was still sorry that it had hurt him.

Jane loved most people, and all dogs, unconditionally. She was genuinely sorry when she couldn't help someone or inadvertently hurt someone. She was sorry for the actions of strangers and for the way humans can treat dogs so badly.

Sorry is such a little word, and said without authenticity it is worse than meaningless, it carries extra pain. But an apology expressed genuinely can soothe and ease pain and strengthen bridges between people.

~ 5 ~

FEELING IN THE MOMENT

Sunset through the trees
E.Goodall (2020)

It's the little things that evoke such strong feelings in me at the moment, and the strangest little things. Some of these feelings sit easily in my heart and soul, whilst others are literally experienced as a large painful lump in my throat. I initially thought that I might have a recurrence of my totally removed thyroid cancer, until someone else told me how they experienced their grief as a lump in their neck/throat. Jane would have told me not to be so silly and then spent half an hour explaining to me why it was so unlikely that my thyroid would grow back, having been totally removed.

My autism helps me to keep my life in neat little boxes most of the time. My whole self is kept in these boxes and I move from one to another depending on context, much like some people have a different handbag for different outfits. For me, my autism also compartmentalizes experiences, memories and a huge amount of information. I imagine my brain like a giant filing cabinet (Mary Poppins could fit a lamppost in her bag, so I can have a metaphorical giant filing cabinet in my head). Some of the filing cabinets are locked and others are familiar and well loved.

The intensity of feelings moment to moment has rendered my boxes and filing cabinets not quite redundant, more too slow to file or box each experience as it occurs. This is both freeing and uncomfortable. It has enabled me to be less contained and far more expressive, but also left me bereft and lost at times.

This morning, it was cold. I got up, fed the dog, Chico, and then went back to bed. Chico snuggled up, taking up as much of the bed as he could and went back to sleep. A while later he woke up and decided to jump up and down all over me and then lick my face. I just felt like he wanted to play so I stuck my hand out of the duvet, which made him leap around even more excitedly. I had a moment of joy in the simple interaction, which was repeated later in the park as he leapt around in the autumn leaves.

The contrast with the horror I experienced today as I watched a car hit a cyclist, the bike fall to the ground and the cyclist arc through the air and then tumble down. I stopped, parked and rushed over to help, forgetting that I can't do anything because it wasn't me that was the Dr. The car had also stopped, the cyclist got up, was able to walk and talk and said he was ok. I went back to the car and bawled. If Dr Jane had been there, she would have insisted on checking him out. I did strongly suggest he go to his GP to get checked out... To see why Dr Jane would have helped see this article from The Press in New Zealand (https://tinyurl.com/yxh4xpce).

Arohanui Jane.

~ 6 ~

A HELPING HAND

Inspired by Dr Jane

Helping hands made a marriage

"If someone needs help or they need something and you can give it to them, then you should."

Jane lived by this creed, giving away her socks to a homeless patient, her shirts to elderly patients, and stopping mid-journey more times than I can count to help out people who needed assistance.

We stopped once to help an elderly lady who was sitting on the pavement. She was clearly confused but gave consent for me to look in her bag whilst Jane checked her physically. The handbag was full of cash and an 'in case of emergency please contact' card. I rang the number and we were given an address to take her.

Jane managed to persuade the lady to get in the car with us and we drove to the address. As Jane was getting the lady out of the car, the door to the home was opened and I was greeted by a middle age man in underpants and nothing else. Her son had come to claim the contents of her handbag...

Whenever Jane was late home it was because she had stopped to help someone or some random dog. Except for one time. This is written about in chapter 8, Late.

~ 7 ~

REACHING OUT

Purple flowers reaching out to the sun
E. Goodall (2019)

Everything is relative, which is an interesting word. I was trying to distract myself from missing my (now dead) wife by watching trashy TV. But what I ended up watching was DIY SOS (Grenfell) (https://www.dailymotion.com/video/x6vkhub), which followed the progress of a new boxing gym being built for the Grenfell community following the horrific fire and loss of life in the Grenfell Towers. It made me think about how, relatively speaking my wife's death was so peaceful and so much less horrific than the experiences of so many within the Grenfell community.

Everyone's grief is valid and different, but for me, I could sit in peace with the death of someone I loved, when that death was instant and painless. It was a timely reminder too, as all the Grenfell locals talked about the importance of healing and moving forward. Not forgetting loved ones, but looking towards the living and supporting those around them. I reflected on how many people are supporting me and how I, in turn, still need to support others, who need support or rely upon me or my input to help them move forward in their lives.

The next day, this relativity was again highlighted during a conversation with a friend. He had come round to see how I was doing, to reach out and offer company, someone to talk with about my wife, about our life. In this reaching out, we connected deeply over our shared attitudes to a variety of social issues. For me, the difficulties he has outweigh my own. I know, when I accept Jane's death as real, that she is never physically coming back. I know that I had something beautiful and precious and now I have the memories. He has memories and hope, a decade of hope. I cannot image the pain and grief involved for all the people with similar journeys. He is cheerful most of the time, has the biggest heart, gentlest personality. But still his journey weighs heavily.

Think about families separated by war or natural disaster or crime, never knowing if or when they might see the rest of their families again. For refugees and asylum seekers in countries that make it almost impossible to become a citizen or even have their claims processed, their fractured lives are rarely thought about or understood. Children who haven't seen parents for years, sibling separated, not knowing if they can ever reconnect, lovers, spouses, all these living on hope, hope that one day they can have back the people they have lost that may still be the people they once knew. And this is where the relative (kin) of relative hit me hardest. I can grieve my loss of kin, knowing it is final, whilst many people are stuck in a (relatively more) tortuous wait of hoping that they can be with their relatives (kin) again.

These two very disparate experiences have helped take the edge off my grief, remind me how much I have had and still have and how much connection between friends, or even relative strangers, can help to ease the burdens that people are carrying on their journey. My challenge to readers this week is to find out how refugees, asylum seekers or victims of natural disasters or violence are supported where you live. Can they fully live or are they getting by on an ever-diminishing hope. Whether you choose to do anything about that or not is up to you, but I have finally understood why Jane used to tell me constantly "helping others eases your own suffering". Kia Kaha

~ 8 ~

LATE

Inspired by Dr Jane

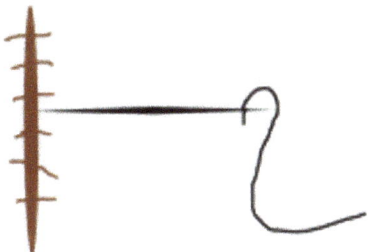

A stitch in time
E.Goodall (2020)

The one-time Jane was late, when it was not because she was helping someone out or just plain distracted, she was covering up someone's mistake. Her mistake.

Jane was an intern then, still working towards her goal of being a doctor. She had stopped working as a psychiatric nurse at night and studying in the day as I insisted she focus on the final goal and that money would be fine (it wasn't really and thank you so much Mark for buying every single item we tried to sell on TradeMe, whether or not you needed it).

Jane had a lipoma and she wanted to get it cut out. She asked a fellow intern, who did it but then freaked out and didn't know how to stitch it up. Jane was carrying around the 'lipoma' so that she could send it to pathology, ever the process follower for *'things that matter'*, when the consultant noticed the giant hole in her arm, packed with gauze.

He stitched it up, she got in a lot of trouble for cutting up her own arm... and I was extremely angry with her when she finally rocked up into the car park where I had been sitting waiting for her for nearly two hours.

~ 9 ~

RECONCILIATION

Woven Koru
E.Goodall (2020) - photo and weaving

This week is National Reconciliation Week in Australia, where I am currently living. As a new Australian, my perspectives may not match many people's. I was lucky enough, not long after becoming a citizen, to attend a 2-day workshop on white privilege. This workshop aimed to help mainly white Australians understand the history of Australia from lived experience perspectives, mainly Aboriginal.

I was stunned at the time that many of my peers did not know, nor have any concept of the events and systemic abuses that followed colonization. Reconciliation requires honesty, which is why the South African process was called Truth and Reconciliation.

However, truth telling is hard work, emotional and painful, and I can see why communities and societies may shy away from such a raw process. As a relative outsider, I knew more of those difficult truths that those born and educated in Australia.

But, perhaps it is my Kiwi connections that grounded me in truly aiming to achieve reconciliation within Australia. Not in a week, and certainly not by setting aside one week of the year to focus on it, but rather by living day to day in ways that validate Aboriginal and Torres Strait Islander experiences as expressed by both individuals and collectively. During the workshop, participants were asked to take a personal stand against racism and to challenge it in their lives. For me in the months since, this has meant asking people not be racist in my home or in my company, blocking people on social media, and not supporting local businesses who have posted racist videos online. I also try to smile at everyone I pass in the street or in a store. This sounds silly but the story that stuck with me most powerfully from the workshop was the one where an Aboriginal Australian felt hurt by the lack of smiles and fleeting contact when out and about, noticing that the white people around her smiled at each other but not at her.

A smile costs nothing, but can be more meaningful than you realise. The only way racism will be defeated is if everyone decides that there is no place for racism in our society. What can you do in your life to challenge racism, whether that is helping those of us who are white understand or responding to those around?

On another note, I am still not reconciled to the facts of life and death, and I am still struggling to accept that my wife will never physically walk through the door again. I am also finding it strange that people offer up ideas as to how fast or slow I should *"move on"*. I am not sure what they mean by this as the dog and I are not planning to move, but the advice often seems to be tinged by judgement;

'not too soon', 'before you get stuck', 'you seem to be doing *very* well, we are *still so sad*'. I often wonder if people think before they assume that just because I am functioning 'very well' at that moment that I am always full of joy?

I also need to reconcile being polite and being respectful with protecting my heart. Kind and generous people who want to share how much they miss Jane and seek to tell me long stories or tell me how irreplaceable she is, even though they have already replaced her as their GP or colleague etc. Here my autism is my gift, I can have my polite mode on, and stand and listen (though I do wonder at people who don't notice the tears running down my face) and then when they take a breath, I can say that "I am sorry I need to leave, it is very sad, Jane was too young and died too soon." Then I go and sit in the car until the tears ease enough for me to drive home.

~ 10 ~

DRIVING

Inspired by Dr Jane

The mobile clinic versus being mobile
E.Goodall (2020)

Jane drove on auto pilot most of the time we were together, only when she become unwell in the last few years, did she try to avoid driving whenever possible. Until for a few months, when she lost the use of one arm, she also temporarily lost her license. Despite not wanting to drive, this devastated her. I bought her a mobility scooter that she could operate one armed, to make sure she could keep as much independence as possible.

Jane had a love-hate relationship with that scooter, seeing it as a manifestation of her new disability. Worrying that people would think she was unable to use her brilliant mind, simply because her body was not working properly.

Early on in our relationship, she was driving me to a dance. We ended up at the hospital where she was training to be a doctor. We got to the dance eventually!

In the last few years, when she had her license, Jane really struggled with driving and I often drove her to her patients after I finished my regular day job. I would wait in the car whilst she did her doctoring and then I'd drive her home. This became a metaphor for our life in times of sickness, each of us on hold for the other whilst handing over the driving and trusting the driver to get us where we needed to go.

~ 11 ~

PERCEPTIONS

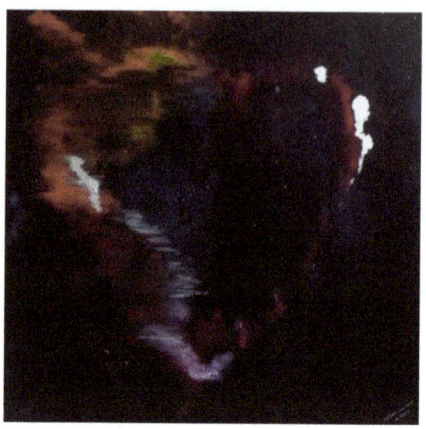

Perceptions (Acrylic painting)
E.Goodall (2018) Artist & photographer

It has been an interesting time in both my micro world and the world at large in the last week. Yesterday I was reminded that people's perceptions as to how I 'should' be feeling 'at this time' after Jane's death. Initially I found it jarring, bordering on offensive, but then I realised that what people are really saying when they think I am 'not sad enough', is that their grief has not been allowed to be expressed in the depth that I have let my grief sit with me.

They mean, your wife touched my life in profound ways that I don't know how to process, nor express adequately. I gently explained to one of her friends yesterday that for me, it is easier to come to terms with her not being here because I am confronted with it multiple times throughout the day and night, every day, without fail. Therefore, I have had to find a way to have that sit with me. The perception may be, that I am not grieving enough, but I honestly don't know how or why people can or would make a judgement on this.

I said to her friend that the hardest time is when I go home from being out anywhere, because that was 'our time', when we would catch up and share our day and just be, be together and be. He gently said that was when the loneliness would kick in, but actually that is just another perception, it is when the sadness kicks in. In my way of being, as an autistic, I tend not to be lonely when I am alone, it is not an emotion that I associate with being alone. Instead, for me loneliness appears when I am in a room full of people with whom I have been unable to connect. I was connected with Jane when we were together and when we were apart, and that connection remains, though I cannot physically be in the same room with her again.

I am not lonely after her death, alone yes, sad yes, devastated yes, connected to her wairua and our friends and whanau, yes. I think that the people who assume that I am not sad enough, do not understand who I am and how I process things, which is ok, but it is a shame that instead of taking the time to actually get to know me, that they feel that a perception of me is enough to pass judgement on me.

Over these two months, I have been reflecting on her life and her achievements, her struggles and the joy and care she brought to so many people; patients, friends, whanau, me. And of course, our dog, who has become a guard dog now, taking his security dog t-shirt that Jane bought him extremely seriously, which would make her both very proud and highly amused.

The other perception that stuck me this week was around humour. A 'joke' was told in my presence, which was met with stony silence from everyone. A joke is only funny and not offensive if both the intent and the delivery are aligned with laughter in mind, and this was a cheap shot that was at best unkind and at worst highly offensive. Interestingly, after a minute the person actually apologised, and seemed to have a lightbulb moment that it really is not ok to say things that can be highly offensive and hurtful. Usually I pull people up on these kinds of behaviours, but I was feeling lonely and that sapped my energy. The other people, just like me, sat and stared at their plates in silence until the apology came, and then the conversation started again.

My perception is that many people are uncomfortable around any type of bigotry, but that they are more uncomfortable with the idea of challenging bigotry. I am not sure why this is, although it is not normally successful as a strategy to end bigotry, based on my experiences vocally challenging people in the past. I have now gained an awareness of the power of silence as judgement, as expression of distaste and disappointment. It seems to offer people a 'face saving' way out that direct confrontation or challenge doesn't.

As you go about your lives this week, perhaps check in with yourself about how you are interacting with others, are you judging based on assumptions and perceptions or on well-founded knowledge? Are you challenging bigotry through conflict or in ways that offer people the opportunity to change without direct confrontation?

~ 12 ~

PERCEPTION

Inspired by Dr Jane

Chico our dog
E.Goodall (2020)

"It is better to be pissed off than pissed on". One of Jane's favourite sayings, the only one our son wanted included in her funeral service. I took a photo of our dog engaged in the act in the park, but chickened out of including that in the service. It is included above. Poor Chico, not sure he'd be that impressed!

Jane was a great believer in 'doing the right thing' and then begging for forgiveness after, if other people, usually her bosses, perceived that it was not the right thing. Often this revolved around her giving people appointments or time that didn't exist. Or starting them on effective medications that had far more paperwork and follow up attached than less effective medications.

Throughout her GP training the only critical feedback from her mentors and examiners was that she needed to be quicker, to be less thorough. Her question to them inevitably left them frustrated: "Who would you like me to cut corners on, whose child or parent or sibling is not important enough?" Many of the critics sent her their own family members, and after she died, many of her patients contacted me to say they have been unable to find a GP as willing to listen, spend time with them and work through complex medical issues.

Jane loved complexity, she loved the challenge of solving those medical puzzles. Her unique mind and encyclopedic knowledge of pharmacology equipping her with the ability to solve all but one of those presenting histories. But not hers. I still do not know why she died. The coroner has finished the investigation. I know it was 'heart or brain'. No shit Sherlock. After years together, listening to her verbalize her thought processes, I have too much medical knowledge and know she died from positional asphyxia. But the cause of death legally is whatever event caused that collapse. The coroner's report is due in another six -nine months.

People perceived that Jane was scatter brained, and she was in so many ways. Her significant ADHD led her to think a thought that led to another to another, before any of these could be thought to completion, her mind had moved on. And yet, in the area of medicine or pharmacology her thoughts were in depth and analytical and her genius in these areas apparent.

I was the one with the invitation to join MENSA, the official genius. She was the one who interpreted the world for me when my autism left me at a loss. I organized her over the years, when she wanted a PA. When she didn't I got grumpy and wouldn't help out, perceiving a slight where there wasn't one.

When she needed my help so intensely, she hated that her body let her down. I hated watching her struggle to do everyday things like eat. It broke both our hearts and we kept that pain to ourselves, preserving the dignity she had left, the perception of normality that leaked out of our lives.

~ 13 ~

SADNESS

Autumn trees. Adelaide.
E.Goodall (2020)

Sometimes the sadness catches me unawares, crashing over me like a tidal wave. I am not sure if it is a sea of consciousness of all that I have lost, or a reaction to the injustices all around, or an over-reaction to someone else's emotions on some light entertainment show or a weird combination thereof. Watching a spark of joy or love brings me a strange mixture of happiness for them and a deep ache that my love is not watching with me. A bit like the way warm grains of sand on the beach feel both comforting and irritating on bare feet.

My interoception (conscious perception of internal body signals, including emotions) is much better than it used to be; a consequence of teaching others how to improve their connections to self. But this is a double edged sword in this time of difficult emotions. As an autistic, I have a naturally analytical and reflective thinking style, that can keep me feeling as if the moment that I am in, will last forever. That I will drown under the tsunami of sadness, without ever making it to another emotion.

To manage this, I rely on reminding myself of two key concepts. For me, these arise out of my Buddhist faith. Although, as a child I used the same logical concepts to manage anxiety or stress.

1. Everything changes
2. Nothing is permanent

Consciously focusing on the fact that the tidal wave cannot be permanent, that it will change, enables me to escape the torrent of grief. In some ways, the being in each fleeting moment, feels like being dragged out to sea and then thrown onto the rocks, but in other ways it is like relaxing on my swing seat, gently swinging back and forward. Jane bought the swing seat for me when I was writing my doctoral thesis. I used to sit and swing with the laptop on my knee, tapping away at the thesis.

I have started swinging again, Chico (our dog), jumps onto my knee and we sit in the dark looking out over the city, gently swinging. And as we swing, the moment is of peace, everything has changed, and will continue to change.

~ 14 ~

TIRED

Inspired by Dr Jane

Jane tired but happy on holiday with Emma in 2019
E.Goodall (2020) 2019

Jane had no interoceptive awareness for her fatigue at all. And I, despite understanding this and having ample evidence; her saying she was not tired and then falling asleep mid-sentence, I was of no support in this at all.

I was angry and frustrated that she would not believe me that I could help and then I gave up trying to help. Except, except, that is not quite true. When really tired, in her last year of life, Jane would collapse and/or lose function on one side of her body. The last neurologist claimed this was due to hemiplegic migraines, who would know.

What I did know was that for the whole of the last year that Jane was alive, I could not go to bed until she was safe in bed. I waited until she was either safe in bed, or I would make sure to get her there once she had collapsed or was unable to move her body as she wanted to.

Until that last night. That night I was so tired, so very, very, tired. I went to bed before Jane. My last words to her were; "I love you, make sure you get to bed safe." She collapsed and died before even making it to bed.

~ 15 ~

STUCK

Adelaide stuck in fog
E.Goodall (2020)

I was reading some of Jane's writing today. She had started her life story numerous times, and once I can work out which bits she wanted to share and which were for us only, I will finish writing it for her. Mixed in with her deep thoughts were notes on how to understand and respond effectively to a range of complex medical issues.

When Jane first met me, I was barely able to move forward, stuck in a horrendous relationship break up in a small town. However, she saw potential in me. To be fair, Jane saw potential in everyone. She had the knack of seeing exactly what people's hidden skills and talents were and guiding them to live in ways that meant those skills and talents were used and grew. This was one of her core purposes in life, to help others achieve their potential.

The raw emotion in Jane's writing caught me unawares. She was a deeply compassionate and kind GP, a caring and big hearted soul who wanted to save all the dogs and old people from any distress.

She would cry at the slightest thing on tv and had the biggest smile, but in general her writing was pharmacology based and humorous or factual. This writing was reflective and carried the pain of years of being stuck when she was younger.

One of our friends said that Jane was one of the kindest people he had ever met, that the world doesn't have many people that kind in it. Ironic that her kindness was born out of prejudice and feeling not good enough. As a child, her ADHD was not understood, she spent most of her education being sent out of class and left school as soon as she could to work with her mum as a cleaner. As a young adult, she realised she was lesbian and had the fear that she would be found out and then faced prejudice that led to her feeling less than.

The pain that years of this brought, was tempered in our 14 years together, but sometimes she would get stuck in her 'less than' pain and I would struggle to bring her back to her beautiful warm smile, filled with love and happiness. Her writing laid bare that pain and the contradictions in life that frustrated her so much. The contradictions of her life and death now frustrate me and Chico struggles to make me get out of bed on the weekend to walk him.

The contradictions are that after a year of worrying about Jane's health, following two week long hospital stays and numerous significant issues, she seemed to be doing much better until a couple of days before she died. Jane was loving helping patients get access to healthcare that had all but disappeared during the pandemic and had finally set up her mobile clinic and was working with her brother on her online stuff. I was driving her around to see patients in the evening once I had finished work, making sure she was safe.

She didn't get covid and I still don't know why or how she died, but she was probably one of the best health care professionals around.

She could work out the diagnosis for someone in an hour, but we had spent a year traipsing around various health professionals to find out virtually nothing. We both knew she was really, really unwell, and we both knew she ran the risk of dying soon, but none of the health professionals seemed to think this.

I can't get stuck in this what if, this pain of what I lost. I need to be in that place of gratitude for what I had, and acceptance that Jane is no longer in pain, no longer suffering. Somehow, reading her pain, which should have reinforced that she is no longer suffering did the opposite. Memories of us laughing, smiling, enjoying life, sharing joy with whanau, everything that is not going to happen again. Jane just adored me and her goals always included having fun in our relationship. This was really hard when she was unwell, when she was so tired, so physically unable to do the everyday things that she wanted. She got stuck for a while in the pain of becoming disabled suddenly, but as was her want, she reinvented herself, taking Chico out on her mobility scooter.

Be kind to people, you don't know if they are stuck, and if so why. People have all kinds baggage that they carry with them, even if they don't choose to share or aren't able to share. Whether a person is a stranger or a partner, we only know what they are able to share. In the last weeks before Jane died, she opened up more than in the previous 14 years and was truly on the path to healing. Ironic. Be patient and kind, if it is clear that someone is stuck, walk alongside them until they are ready and able to move forward too.

~ 16 ~

DON'T GET STUCK

Inspired by Dr Jane

Jane had told me a number of times before she died, not to get stuck in grief, to move on, to have another relationship, to keep doing the work I do etc etc. She so desperately wanted my possible grief experience to be so different to hers.

When her mum died, Jane looked after her to the very end, then slept in the room for the week of the wake. She grieved heavily for five years. For much of that time, she was lost in her grief, stuck in a place of sadness, except for when she was helping others. When helping she came alive and could be in the present moment fully.

Ganesh at Night - Bali
E.Goodall (2019)

I understand why she got stuck, her loss was huge. She frequently described herself as her "*mum's right arm*". We once spent the whole day pruning roses for her mum, because otherwise 'they will turn to hawthorns tomorrow.' Not sure Jane nor I actually knew what hawthorns were.

Jane also got stuck in her perception that she should be the family provider, financially. I was the emotional rock in her head, even when I could not see how she felt supported and stable because I was in her life. She wanted me (and our son) to be financially taken care of when/should she die. She became obsessed by this when she was unable to work. Which broke my heart, as we had never focused on money.

She rarely charged her patients and gave away our belongings regularly. But her need to 'care take' was so strong. When she loved, she loved so deeply, so strongly. Her heart was so expansive, she loved many, many, people and every dog! She bought and distributed dog food for strays, left water down outside wherever she worked in the Northern Territory and paid vet bills for dogs that might otherwise be euthanized. At one stage we were spending more on dogs than on our own bills. She needed to help when she could.

~ 17 ~

LAUGHTER (OR LACK OF)

Chico the source of much laughter
E.Goodall (2020)

I know what I miss the most, the silliness, the laughter and love filling the house. Instead, if there is a moment of play with Chico, it is instantly followed by the stark awareness that the echo of another's laughter will not bounce into the space. That the light-hearted moments that bring laughter into life, heart and home are on hold.

People are reluctant to visit, they miss the presence of my advice-giving wife. They will come in briefly and leave with awkward kindness. There are exceptions, people who will share a meal, sit on the deck, cuddle the dog. When laughter comes out of joy, it is healing of heart, mending of relationships, and caressing of the soul.

Many years ago, a friend stayed with us and was astounded by how natural and authentic both Jane and I were, in our home and with each other. Part of that authenticity was lots of silliness. Jane used humour to educate and share her skills and knowledge and I use, or rather used to use, silliness to de-stress, to bring some joy and laughter to both of us. When we were dating, Jane said jokingly that she didn't like giggly 'girts', then kissed me and said that she loved me. We shared a love of learning, knowledge and trying to make the world a better place, which can be heartbreaking and hard. And we shared laughs and giggles, silly dances and singing to manage that heartbreak.

Now the heartbreak is mine alone, though shared with others who have loved and lost. The laughs stop short of real and have no power to heal. People think that kindness is only gentle and fleeting, but it sometimes needs to be intense and filled with laughter.

I don't understand many people's jokes. My autism brings with it some interesting communication difficulties that are not easily visible and often misunderstood. Much like my inability to get most people's humour, learning as a child to laugh when the people around laughed. As a young adult, I discovered that some people got me and I understood them, I could laugh with them, not behind them.

Jane similarly found her tribe eventually, found her home, where her heart could be heavy or light and she was still understood and loved, and cajoled into laughing and dancing or singing. We were a tribe of three, though we teased our son that he was only number two or three son (depending on how many dogs we had), and he had left home leaving just the fur kid and us.

Jane bought the tiny fur kid a t-shirt with 'security dog' written on and joked about his security dog skills. Currently, he doesn't even need the t-shirt to be a guard dog. Jane would be so proud. He springs around the park like a weird rabbit, which brings me a smile. When Jane was really ill and couldn't work, she grew fond of the tiny dog. He made her smile when she was struggling, just like he does for me now.

As she got better, she would play with him, just as I do now, and small giggles of joy would erupt, then be echoed back as my heart filled with joy, seeing Jane laughing and leaping around with Chico. Take those minute moments of everyday happiness and really be present for them, for when they are gone, if you were not present, your memories will be lesser, and your life less rich that it could have been.

~ 18 ~

MOULD ON CHEESE

Inspired by Dr Jane

The Breakaways (nr Coober Pedy, SA)
E.Goodall (2019)

Before I physically met Jane, she told me that she grew on people like mould on cheese. We met online, on the Pink Sofa, while Jane was working nights and I was trying to survive a seriously unpleasant break up in a country I had only lived in for a few months, whilst working in a job that was less than ideal. I am allergic to cheese mould! So, it was a good job it was a metaphor. Not sure I ever understood it, but I did notice that most people liked her more and more, the more time they spent with her. If, and it is a big if, if they shared some of the same values as her. If not, the more time they spent with her, the less time she wanted to spend with them. I am sure it was probably mutual.

Jane was extremely outgoing when I met her. She would throw big parties for her med school friends and the mental health nurses that she worked with. I was extremely shy and didn't drink alcohol. Her friends were invariably lovely and could drink copious amounts of alcohol, get very drunk and still help clean up before they went home.

Jane once jumped into the river to save me after a bunch of drunk nurses convinced me to sit in a kayak and then pushed the kayak off the riverbank and into the river. As the tide was out it was a big drop. I fell out, my glasses fell off and I had no idea what to do. Jane jumped in, held me up and we swam the few metres to shore. Sopping wet, Jane then paid someone $10 to jump in and search for my glasses, as without them, I have very poor vision and can get highly anxious. And now, I can tell everyone that an All Black rescued my glasses. (He is an All Black now, he was a teenager then).

Jane's med school friends learnt that she had met this 'woman with really interesting pathologies', before they actually met me. They would give her lecture notes if she as late to class, having worked a night shift prior. They would hang out on our 'grass' by the river bank when they had a few weeks off. Jane was at peace with these people, none of whom were typical medical students. Moving away from New Zealand was hard for Jane. She found it harder to make friends. I, who had always been super shy, and hadn't even wanted to move initially, made friends more easily and loved most of the jobs I got.

Interestingly, many of the people in Australia who liked Jane, did not like me. They only saw our differences, whereas my friends and our kiwi friends and whanau saw both our similarities and our differences.

~ 19 ~

BLOSSOM

Spring Blossom - Adelaide SA
E.Goodall (2020)

There is a tree on one of the walks that the dog and I do, that is unexpectedly in blossom (see photo on left). It is beautiful. Blossoms have an emotional significance for me, and these blossoms reminded me of the cherry blossom in Japan. Jane had taken me to see Japan and we had timed it perfectly and got to see the blossoms from Tokyo right down to Hiroshima.

It was an interesting trip, people were so kind and helpful and then there was the person who was so excited to see me that their hand

and arm moved uncontrollably and his hand slapped me. I smiled gently at this stranger, who was so excited and then Jane and I carried on with our day.

The chef who made these special ramen in chilli oil, and as we sat in his tiny ramen bar, I struggled to eat a food that I often love and the chef handed me a fizzy drink 'to help with the chilli'. I was so touched by his thoughtfulness that I ate the ramen and drank the fizzy. I hate fizzy. I got to eat from a bento box on the 'bullet train' and like the over excited autistic that I was, I was as happy flappy as could be for the entire train ride.

The amazing food in tiny ryokan, sleeping in traditional Japanese style. Jane asking for as many spare futon mattresses as possible so she could feel more comfortable, whilst ending up looking like the Princess and the pea. This made me laugh so much as I am the Princess and the Pea, not able to sleep if there is one breadcrumb or lump in the bed!

Blossoms can be brief or long lived, they come and then they drop off the tree with the wind or rain, or they die and fall off. Lives are brief or long, people come into your life and then they are gone. But like blossoms, people can bring moments of joy and beauty both when they are there and when they are gone. The memory of the form behind the joy and beauty is almost as tangible as the experience.

I am finding moments of focus and drive, reconnecting with friends and interests in brief moments like short lived blossoms. Work got us all to do an online art class and I enjoyed painting again. Now I am one step closer to using the canvases Jane bought me earlier in the year, reminding me gently that I should keep doing the things that bring me peace, and not just focusing on doing things. Chico nudges me to walk him when he is bored, and I find scraps of paper with thoughts Jane had scrawled down randomly, briefly blossoming into a writer before drifting back to her passion for health.

The way my autistic brain processes life and as it turns out death, is both helpful and difficult. What I discovered this week, is that this is the same for everyone, everyone finds some things hard and other things easy. The guy who borrowed a coffee cart to try and make a living during covid, was asking me about how he could support his friend, whose wife just unexpectedly died, because he knows my wife died. He wanted to help, but didn't know how.

I made myself late for a work meeting, because it felt important to have a real conversation with him, to hear his pain for his friend, and share some things that had helped me. And in that moment, I understood that grief and loss can be like blossom, when it appears, it takes up your attention, and holds it with a delicate fragility that gets buffeted by the winds of memory and the rains of sorrow.

So many people are being buffeted by memories, both joyous and difficult, and the rains of sorrow, grief and loss or the anticipation of these. Be kind and gentle to those you interact with, bring them some moments of peace or calm or genuine helpful human connection.

~ 20 ~

CONNECTION

Inspired by Dr Jane

Sunset at Moana Beach SA
E.Goodall (2020)

"*Seek to understand*", Jane gently and not so gently changed the way I interacted with others, removed the remnants of my judgmental attitudes, and taught me to question more than I already did. When someone was mean, she would point out there would be a reason that might not justify what they did, but it would explain it. And this explanation, would change a response.

Jane connected deeply with so many people, even if she only had a few hours of contact with them. Following her death, literally hundreds of people contacted me to say how she had changed their lives. Some were more expected and obvious than others; the people whose lives she literally saved.

By far and above the most common sentiment was that Jane has listened to them in ways that no-one else ever had. We had this in common, both of us able to listen without judgement to the journeys that people were on. So many people studied nursing and/or pharmacology because of the way she talked about and taught these topics. Jane loved nursing and nurses. I never failed to find it ironic that I dropped out of nursing after killing the resuscitation dummy during my first aid exam.

Jane connected from the heart, genuinely wanting to know the people she interacted with, whether as their doctor or their friend.

~ 21 ~

BROKEN RECORD/ PERSEVERATION

Sunset caught on the blind
E.Goodall (2020)

So, this broken record thinking of mine, is a very typical autistic thinking style. In psychology and psychiatry, this fixated repetitive thinking is called perseveration. It is not thought of as a good thing. And yet, despite this being my default thinking style, I would not dream of phoning someone five times in one day, especially when the voicemail says that the phone owner is dead. This week, an unnamed streaming service provider phoned Jane twice on one day and five times the next.

Obviously, her credit cards have been cancelled, the banks do not offer credit to people who are dead.

I did not listen to the messages, I couldn't bring myself to. The reason her voicemail says she is dead was that I knew her patients would be calling her when she didn't show up for appointments or call them with blood test results and I didn't know how to tell them of our loss, her death. It may not have been the most sensitive thing to do, but it was the only logical thing I could think of to do. I could not bring myself to answer her phone and that anxiety was bigger than the loss of hearing her voice if I called her phone. I wish I had been braver.

Anyway, the streaming service had a serious case of broken record, once I found out that was who it was by googling the phone number. I called them to cancel the service, which I had planned to take over. They don't deserve my custom, insensitive to the last second of the call. I have hardware that needs returning, but no way to return it as they wanted the account number to provide the return label and I don't have the account number, which I did explain. In their incredibly obtuse manner, they explained that Jane would be fined if she did not return the box within a week. Good luck with that!

I am finally fixating once again on my interoception thesis, holding my love for, and memories of, Jane in my heart as I type away. She spent an inordinate amount of time telling me to keep doing what I do, keep working on making the world a better place, being kind and caring. So, I shall do as I was told, which for those of you who know me personally, know is a rare thing indeed. My broken record thinking is at the heart of my interoception research, the core of my ability to work through all the threads of an issue to problem solve the insolvable. Jane worked through the medical issues of her patients in the same way, going over and over all the details until she could see how they linked.

Perhaps in time, it will be understood that most ways of being have pluses and minuses, strengths and support needs. Both of our thinking styles caused problems for us, separately and as a couple, at times. But we both made careers out of our problem-solving strengths, held tightly in a grip of kindness and valuing of the people that we worked with.

When you are interacting with others, or even yourself, this week, be patient and thoughtful. If the way they do something annoys you, pause and see the strengths as well as the support needs, the pluses as well as the minuses. One of the earliest lessons that Jane gifted to me was; "seek to understand." She was right, behind every action, or lack thereof, word or moment of being ignored, there is at least one story. When we understand the story it may not excuse what happened, but it may well explain it.

The picture is the sunset captured through the blind, not yet visible anywhere else. I love watching the sunset, often taking a photo to send to friends and family or post online. I miss sharing them with Jane, arohanui Jane.

~ 22 ~

TECHNOLOGY

Jane with cables and plugs
E.Goodall (2019)

Inspired by Dr Jane

Jane had an interesting relationship with technology. She loved using the computer to 'find a bargain', which was how we ended up with a thousand otoscopes when we couldn't afford food on the table. She often didn't notice texts but did check emails. She felt compelled to answer phone calls no matter the time of day or night, but would leave emails and texts unanswered for months at a time.

Destroying stuff was something Jane loved, give her a hammer and she would smash it. Building things, not so much interest. But creating PowerPoints to teach pharmacology or medical error would have her hunched over the laptop for hours and hours, joyfully editing pictures and complex diagrams to impart difficult topics with humour.

I had bought her speech to text software as she typed really slowly, and it frustrated her so much. When we wrote books together, I would interview her and then type her answers up and submit the book before she got a chance to say how much it needed editing. Jane was a perfectionist, who struggled to finish anything written on the computer, as it could still be improved. I am a 'submitted is better than not' person. I was a perfectionist as a child, but my English teacher destroyed any vestiges of perfectionism.

Jane who left school young, with few formal qualifications and a hatred of teachers, married one (me), loved learning and sharing her knowledge and grew ever more perfectionist over the years. I was most impressed when Jane spent hours learning how to do things with her laptop as she thought she should be able to. Propped on the sofa with her phone charger and laptop, she used technology to teach herself to cook, when she decided that if she wasn't working and I was, that maybe she should cook dinner for us in the evenings.

Going into the kitchen, Jane would have a video recipe open and do each step at a time, pause, and then continue. This led to a number of revelations and put an end to her complaints when I made something that was only marginally edible. Cooking was less easy than she had assumed after years of eating porridge for every meal and drinking first pepsi max and then solo.

~ 23 ~

ONE FOR SORROW, TWO FOR JOY

Two magpies at home
E.Goodall (2020)

    This is the beginning of a longer rhyme, often recited in response to sightings of magpies. Since Jane, my wife, died, I have been ever so slightly obsessed with this rhyme. In the first few days, I only ever saw one magpie, and the universe seemed to be reinforcing my sorrow. Endless grey skies with unseasonable rain accompanied endless lone magpies.

Over the following months, Adelaide has returned to the mainly sunny winter days that we both loved, and as Chico, the dog, and I, walk around our streets, we see. We see the singular blossom hidden in a barren tree, an elderly man planting a rose bush gifted by his neighbour, and a second magpie hiding nearby whenever we see a sole sorrowful magpie.

I wondered if the universe was telling me, that wherever there is sorrow, there is also joy in hiding, waiting to be discovered. Maybe not today, or tomorrow, or even this year or next. Maybe the joy is in tiny doses, split seconds within the sorrow, containing a spark of 'not sorrow'. Like the single flower blooming in the winter sun. We, Chico and I, rarely see a single magpie now. Three months have passed and the sorrow has settled into the ground on which we walk.

I had thought sorrow might be a cloak, but the magpie pairs, swooping and dancing with each other in the air, remind me that sorrow and joy are not two sides of the same coin, that neither can be a cloak that captures the wearer. Rather they are reflections of the soul and the mind in the moment. If I stay in the moment, and look, truly look at the blossoms, at the concentration of the elderly man planting the rose, and the playing magpies. I see both their joy and the sorrows that have gone before and may come again.

Everyone and every creature experiences loss, it is not unique to me. Loss can be fleeting, a grain of sand lost from the beach to the ocean, or massive like the bushfires that devastated huge swathes of Australia early in the year, racing up cliffs and over roads, destroying everything it its path. In loss, with time there are inevitable changes. The coastline changes shape and the regrowth of ash fuelled country will occur after enough rain.

I talk to the elderly man when he is out in his garden. Chico bounds up and down like a puppy in the winter grass in the park. We met a lady whose home of sixty odd years was being sold and subdivided, and spent some time listening to her loss and pain. The trees she spent time among, with her father, will soon be gone, as he is long gone. Validating her sorrow, I wished her moments of joy in her journey forward.

Take time in your busy days, to be that moment of joy, or that possibility of shared sorrow easing a sorrow that was held before by one. There is no infinite sorrow, nor infinite joy, instead there are moments that could be lengthy or moments that could be infinitesimally short. Be present for the moments of joy, no matter how short and know that the moments of sorrow shall end eventually.

One for sorrow,
Two for joy,
Three for a girl,
Four for a boy,
Five for silver,
Six for gold,
Seven for a secret,
Never to be told.

~ 24 ~

LOSS

Jane's treasured gift from her mum
E.Goodall (2020) photo only

Inspired by Dr Jane

Jane felt things deeply, mostly the difficult emotions. The news would make her cry in despair, whilst I refused to watch the problems of the world played out on our screens, she engaged with her whole heart. She really struggled with loss of any kind. Her big heart would hold the pain and grief and hold it tight.

So tight is tried to eat her up to escape. The death of our German Shepherd hurt her very being. I was so much more pragmatic; he had been suffering terribly and had no quality of life anymore. She just missed him; the loss palpable in her very being.

Jane had so much loss. She often talked about not being able to cope with anymore, that she did not know what she would do if we ever broke up. She even found it hard to let our son leave home, her love for him burning bright in their phone conversations and our visits together.

Jane didn't want to have regrets when someone died. She worked really hard to make sure that her parents were happy with her, just in case they died. And when they did, one years before the other, she could say hand on heart, that she did everything she could for them.

In her dying, she lost me and I lost her. I think she must have known she was going to die, even if it was subconscious. The night before I hadn't slept, having a strong premonition that she was about to die. When she was alive in the morning, I felt silly and allowed myself that one early night. She, she spent the perfect last day with me. I can look back and say it was the perfect last day.

She gave me that gift. Made that loss as considerate as possible. Although I will never forget how I found her, and the pointless CPR I performed waiting for the ambulance. She was already dead, and I knew that. I am trained in advanced first aide. The ambulance people knew that, but she was the Dr for a patient they took to hospital a few months before and they knew she had saved that patient's life, so they tried really hard.

I temper these memories of the way I lost her, with the peace on her face when they took all their machines away and told me to say goodbye. The peace that sat within her body when we held the funeral. I know she could not have been able to manage losing me. I have no choice but to manage. Our son needs a mother and I love him as much as she did.

~ 25 ~

LONELY VERSUS ALONE

A single group of blossoms on a bare tree
E.Goodall (2020)

An interesting thing about autistics, is that many of us are very acutely aware of the difference between being lonely and alone. It is of course possible to be both, but on the whole being alone doesn't bother me, besides which I am not alone, I have Chico. As many other autistics and other animal lovers will attest, pets, in my case a dog, truly do provide a lot of company.

I remember before I met Jane, one one of my predominant emotions when at a social event was loneliness, and being lonely in a room full of people is a difficult emotional place to be. You can see other people connecting and seeming to enjoy their interactions. In contrast, I would find a quiet space to sit or stand, often nursing an almost empty glass, realizing too late that there wasn't anything to drink that wasn't alcoholic. Once I met Jane, that changed, she would remind me to take juice if that was what I wanted to drink. She would tell me that we could leave as soon as I wanted to, and if I wanted to stay home instead, I could.

Why would someone who felt uncomfortable in social situations, put themselves in those situations? I can't speak for anyone else, but I did it because I didn't know that I didn't have to. Interestingly, I have never felt uncomfortable teaching in a room full of students, whether they were adult or child students. A staff room is a very different thing, though over the years there have been a few that offered genuine acceptance and warmth to everyone, myself included.

As Jane's love of people, watching people, talking with people, seeking to understand people, became part of the fabric of my life, I started to realise, that I was just me, and me is ok just as I am. I was less lonely in a room full of people, and never lonely when I was with Jane. But that legacy of loneliness and disconnect, lingers in my comfort in a room without other people. Don't get me wrong, I love being with my friends and whanau, when I can be completely me, with no strange looks if I tic or stutter, things that happen when I am tired or anxious.

Perhaps after I got my autism diagnosis, I understood my discomfort and accepted my disconnect with people I don't know well as just as it is, and not an indictment on some unknown personality flaw. This acceptance led to a greater willingness to say no to events I didn't want to attend and a greater capacity to attend ones that Jane really wanted. Many of which comprised either med students, junior doctors and/or psychiatric nurses depending on which stage of her med training she was in. All of whom were lovely, my favourite being the pysch nurses, who would wash up and clean and tidy before leaving. Even the ones who launched me in a kayak into the river after the tide had gone out, were so warm and inclusive.
I think what I learnt from this is that I am probably not the only person who can and does feel lonely around other people, and that how I act can be the difference for someone else that Jane and the pysch nurses were for me. This means that when I interact with someone, I try to set them at ease, I try to genuinely see them, be welcoming to them in voice and heart. I do not need everyone to like me, but I do not want to contribute to anyone else's discomfort or anxiety. I think Jane was so warm to people for many of the same reasons,

wanting to set people at ease in ways that were not afforded to her when she was younger.

I do not understand unkindness between or towards individuals. The world is hard enough as it is, why contribute negativity? I love that I was able to bring Jane some joy, when she said she wanted to locum in the outback or remote Islands, I always said go for it, when she wanted to set up a new way of being a GP, I said go for it. This support of her dreams made her very happy, because she rarely put herself first. I am much less outgoing but more more adventurous, risk averse in areas Jane was not (money) and not in areas that she was (writing, cooking). Over the years we evened those areas out a bit and her outback experiences brought her a lot of joy and connection.

These were jobs were she spent the evening and night alone, as I rarely travelled with her when she was on a locum. She should have been lonely, and she did indeed miss me terribly when she was away, but she always connected with the community. Jane was an incredibly gifted GP, who wanted to share her gift with people who may not always get access to medical practitioners who genuinely care, who truly saw them and valued them.

When we genuinely see people, and hold them in our hearts and voices with care and kindness, we can disagree with grace, or agree with joy. As you interact with others this week, try to truly see them, their journey to this moment in time, their pain and sorrow, their joy and happiness. You may feel pleased to be around them, you may not, but in turn, they may or may not be pleased to be themselves. In times that I have not been comfortable in myself, I have not been as kind to others as I should. Jane helped me to be a better me, and this is a great legacy to leave, even if it is just one person, but for her it was nearly everyone she met. I may not be that gracious, but I can try and so can you.

~ 26 ~

LONELY WHEN ALONE

Jane with a rescue roo. Outback Australia
From Jane's phone - taken by the chopper pilot (2018)

Inspired by Dr Jane

Jane was a locum GP in remote and outback Australia and a locum Psychiatric Dr around regional Australia and New Zealand for many years. She absolutely loved this work, but was always so lonely when alone after hours.

She wanted me to travel with her, to share the experiences that she found so special. Occasionally I did, but not often, as I worked full-time and ran a business too. When I travel, I am not lonely, I write in the evenings and watch rubbish on TV to distract my busy mind.

I was Jane's distraction for her busy mind. Her ADHD kept her thoughts racing when she wasn't at work. I can't do one thing at a time, I watch tv whilst writing, listen to the radio whilst reading a book. Jane could only do one thing at a time, not even have a conversation whilst watching tv. This meant talking with me interrupted her chaotic never-ending busy thought machine.

And she loved me, she knew she was safe with me, that I cared. That I admired her intelligence, loved her generous heart and was happy to listen to her music and that I loved her too. After Grace killed herself when Jane was away on a locum, and I had to tell her over the phone, Jane travelled less. And when she travelled less, she noticed how much I travelled for work. And then she was lonely when she was alone at home.

Being kind and generous to others helped her combat her loneliness. She loved her final job as a GP in an aged care home, with patients/residents who all had dementia. She loved those patients so much, giving them hours of her time, to just sit and chat and bring them some joy.

She took the ones who liked chocolate, chocolate. Candy for the ones who preferred candy and then she brought me along so that I could take Chico around to visit the residents. Her heart broke for the people who had no visitors. When covid forced a lock down, she saw her patients nearly every day until she died, to make sure they were not lonely nor alone.

Jane understood how insidious loneliness is, how it can eat at your spirit until you are lost. I know that I helped keep her grounded, staving off the depths of despair, but I could not be there all the times that she wanted me to be. Or I could have if I had made different choices. Or she could have been there with me when I travelled, if she had made different choices.

~ 27 ~

A LIFETIME AGO

Heart in a tree
E.Goodall & K.Kenah
(2018)

I love words, the sound of them, the way they dance in my mind. But some phrases bring me to a stand still, they punch my soul and my heart feels suspended in time. This is one of them. When someone casually said that something felt life it was 'a lifetime ago', it was all I could do not to blurt out; 'yes, it was, Jane's lifetime ago.'

I know it is just a phrase, I know it means, it feels like a long long time ago. But I equally know the power of words to heal or to hurt. When we use words casually, without thought, our throw away sounds can cause pain, when we did not mean to. I am usually aware that I do not know where other people are on their journey through life, I do not know what sorrow or hurt they are carrying.

I have a friend who prefaces some sentences with; 'I don't mean any offense' or 'I can't find the right way to say this.' They do this to prevent offense or judgement and I appreciate their openness with their communication struggles. Many people I know communicate more carefully or more openly and honestly because of their autism. I try to be both careful and honest in my words and I have a strong preference to be friends with people who are also careful and honest or open.

Part of that carefulness, was not responding to those three words that meant such different things to the speaker and to me, the listener. Jane's lifetime ago is a three and a half months ago. Jane's lifetime ago, I had a wife, a life-partner, a best friend and the world had one more amazing selfless person. Jane's lifetime ago, I was one half of Emma-and-Jane or Aunty Jane-and-Aunty Emma. Now, I may wear a wedding ring (her ring) but I do not have a wife, there is no Emma-and-Jane, there is just an Emma.

In this lifetime, this is not my first loss and will not be my last, loss is a part of life. But it is my first loss that changed my status, wife to widow, part of a pair that was seen as 'one' by so many, to the left behind part. The first where language is painful. I have not used the word widow a second time, until this post. It hurt too much the last/first time.

Whilst so many people are suffering in this world, at this time, I think I am going to be even more careful in the use of words. I don't want to inadvertently cause pain to someone who may be struggling with their physical or mental health or their anxiety for someone else's. Stay as safe as you can, be kind to those around and think about how your words, that you may think are casual throw-aways, may impact those around you.

kia kaha

~ 28 ~

KIA KAHA (STAY STRONG)

Fall down seven times, stand up eight.

One of Jane's favourite sayings from Japan

Inspired by Dr Jane

We were in Christchurch, New Zealand when the big earthquakes started. We lost homes and Jane lost a colleague to the damage. Kia kaha became a phrase that was incorporated into the lives of many Cantabrians during those scary times. Jane integrated it into her philosophy of kaizen (continuous improvement) and the Japanese proverb; fall down seven times, stand up eight.

When Jane faced a barrier to her continuous improvement, she would find a way to circumvent it, driven in her desire to better herself and give her family a good life. Jane got a place at medical school after failing to get in, when as a nurse she accurately diagnosed an elderly patient's condition and the consultant decided that Jane should become a doctor.

When we met, Jane told me she came with; elderly parents, a son. and a brother with Down's syndrome and that it was a package deal. If I wasn't interested, could I please walk away. I came with a big dose of distress as my eleven-year relationship had just ended with my partner becoming involved with two of my colleagues in a small town primary school. I was devastated that all the parents, of my students, knew! I moved out into my own house but struggled to do anything other than work and eat fish and peas for dinner.

I came with six chickens and a crazed 2-year-old bichon frise that I bought to keep me company. Unfortunately, Buddy was a puppy mill dog, who had only ever lived in a kitchen cupboard with mesh for a door. He ran away all the time and peed on everything.

Jane gave me my strength and confidence back. She loved me for who I was, autistic and book smart. Useless at giving driving directions and remembering my medications but highly organised with everything else. She reminded me how much I loved learning and was so proud when I got my PhD. I encouraged her to follow her passions and seek out her joy. She was the first person from Australia or New Zealand to do the British Association of Psychopharmacology qualifications, travelling to the UK several times over the years to complete this.

After her dad died, and I nearly died as she was by his side in New Zealand and I was in the emergency room in South Australia, after that I pushed her to do whatever she wanted. She had done job after job because it made her parents happy, and it paid for things for all the people she and we supported. Now, I earn enough, we had enough, and I felt she deserved to have that time to explore what it was that she wanted. Some jobs only lasted a few weeks. I didn't care and I helped her not to see this as failure, but to see it for what it was, exploring what she wanted to do.

She found what she wanted to do. In the month before she died. Jane found her contentment in her work. She set up a mobile GP clinic to home visit patients, at a time when covid was closing down access to face to face GP services. Often I drove her, after I finished my main job during the day. Sometimes she drove herself. She also continued to work at the aged care home as the GP for some of the patients/residents with dementia and she loved the patients. Sometimes I would visit with her, with Chico. We couldn't do this when covid forced the lockdown, which made her sad.

She also had a third job as a GP at a pharmacy not far from home, where she was vaccinating people and providing a walk in GP clinic. After her death, the pharmacy staff told me repeatedly how valued she was by their clients.

Jane got to practice medicine how she wanted in that month. Having variety of places in which she worked, with no access barriers for her patients. I wanted her to work less. I told her she was killing herself by working too much. I told our son that I thought she would die during covid. She told me that it would kill her not to work.

I accepted her choice and I know she was right. It was better for her to live a shorter more productive life. And I loved her, so I wanted what was right for her. Whether or not it was right for me is not relevant. Kia kaha to all those who have to face these decisions.

~ 29 ~

EXHAUSTION

Moana Beach, SA.
E.Goodall (2020)

Grief and loss are exhausting. Today would have been Jane's birthday. She would have been 56. Normally I would have woken her up with a card and a present if she was home and I was home, if not with a phone call. Instead, I went to the beach to collect pebbles. Jane would bring me pebbles from her trips, knowing how how much I love their textures and colours.

About 8 or 9 years ago, Jane and I went to Fox Glacier, the 25 minute walk to the glacier took us an hour because I kept stopping to take photos of rock striations and various pebbles. I took 1 photo of the glacier. It was a great trip, we sat in the hot pools in the town as the stars came out and the rain fell. Magic.

A colleague sent me flowers today, to remember Jane and let me know of their care and support. One of Jane's exes sent me a lovely text. I am gently held from afar by so many hands of care, many of whom I first met through Jane, but some of whom are my tribe, my autistic friends and whanau, and some of whom I have never met, but for whom Jane was so special.

I got home from the beach and Chico wanted to go for a walk. I could hear Jane's voice in my head as I ummed and ahhed (it was cold and raining). "Don't be mean, take the little fluffy thing for a walk, he was so good to me when I wasn't well." He got his walk, we got wet. We saw three pairs of beautiful green and red birds, gorgeous red buds filling tree branches that were bare yesterday.

Each and every sad moment is like the sky at the beach today, heavy clouds of sadness, through which the light or moments of joy shine, when you least expect it. Nothing is forever, sadness, happiness, life. I am so appreciative of the gifts of wisdom and love that Jane so freely gave and I am truly a better person for having had her in my life. At the same time, I know I was often the light when she had clouds and that she was able to be the best her that she could be in the years we were together.

I gave her the gift of acceptance, I had no issue with her ADHD, her wish to change jobs so frequently, often after 6 weeks. Admittedly, I wasn't so understanding about the 1000 otoscopes she bought during 5th year med school, "because they were a good deal". I gave away the last of them in the weeks after her death, they went to good homes.

I gave her the gift of believing in her, valuing her skills and respecting her values (which we shared, though she was far more generous than me). Jane had finally come into her own, practicing medicine exactly how she wanted to – taking time and care with each patient, educating them so they could be active participants in their healthcare. I was so proud of her, even though we both joked that she was the poorest GP in Australia because she wouldn't charge her patients and the government disproportionately financially rewards what she termed 'checkout operator medicine.'

Neither of us cared about the money, we had enough, we were content to make a difference in the lives of the people we interacted with. On this, your first not here anymore birthday Jane, I want you to know how proud I still am of you and that you are forever in my heart and in my mind. I am still trying to live the values we shared, and I promise to keep walking Chico even if it rains, because it never rains forever. Arohanui Jane.

~ 30 ~

PAIN IS EXHAUSTING

Jane and I. Jane exhausted and unwell, but very happy on our holiday celebrating our first wedding anniversary and 11th civil union anniversary.
E.Goodall (2019)

Inspired by Dr Jane

Jane had chronic pain for all her adult life. As a child she injured her knee during a judo competition. The surgery to fix it left her in constant pain and ended her judo career.

Then a horse that she was riding fell and the horse stood on and kicked Jane when trying to get up, leaving Jane with a serious crush injury on her 'good leg'. This injury caused significant pain and discomfort for the rest of her life.

Other things that contributed to her constant pain:

- Gall bladder – removed as defective and causing pain and other issues
- Kidney – stones caused pain and discomfort, and then it ruptured and she had to be airlifted from the outback to hospital
- Large teratoma on her ovary – significant issues requiring an urgent hysterectomy
- Multiple pulmonary emboli – nearly killed her and caused extreme fatigue
- Raised intra-ocular pressure that nearly left her blind
- Hemiplegic migraines – caused left sided paralysis and/or loss of function in the evenings and overnight

Etc etc etc Jane was exhausted for the last few years of her life. It was her normal and it sucked for her and it sucked to watch.

~ 31 ~

ANXIETY

Landscape with clouds at sunrise. Australia
E.Goodall (2020)

I am quite happy to admit, anxiety sucks, my anxiety sucks. I have no experience of anxiety without autism, but as someone who is autistic, I intimately understand anxiety in the context of autism. Having said that, I rarely admit I have anxiety, not out of shame or fear, but out of denial and a lack of interoceptive awareness of anxiety.

What this means is I do not notice anxiety building and I may not even be aware that I am anxious. It is only when I haven't slept properly for more than three days and/or my repetitive thinking is completely focused on one or two things that it will slowly dawn on me that I am anxious about that one or two things.

When you can't sense anxiety building, you can't address it in its infancy. Instead you can only respond to the tempestuous teenager of anxiety, a full-on emotion that has all the logic and manageability of teen hormones. Even then I may not be able to tell the difference between stress and anxiety. In both, thoughts go round and round in ever deeper cycles of analysis.

In a moment of realization that deeper cycles are still merely repetitions with no value or help, I reached out to a friend to talk through the issues. Which, unlike many of the issues over my life that have provoked anxiety, are not so trivial that there were not worthy of any more thought. These were vaguely big issues, worthy of in-depth conversation that, with both parties being autistic, wound a path of logic and analysis.

In the end, I was reminded of something that I have taught kids over all my years in education. "It is ok if you don't know, it's ok to not be sure. It's ok to just try something. You won't know if something is right (or not) for you, unless you actually try it." Take eggplant, hated it for years, such a horrible texture, with the skin and the inside touching but completely different. Then one day, I tried it when it was barbecued, yum!

Obviously, or maybe not so obviously, some things should never be tried. Ones that may hurt you or someone else or the environment. I can't claim that eating eggplant could hurt someone else or the environment. It has physically and emotionally hurt me in the past though!

When we are hard on ourselves, expecting perfection in our behaviour and reactions. When we think that we are grownups who shouldn't still be stumbling through life, learning skills, consolidating knowledge, we do ourselves a disservice. We need to to be as kind to ourselves as we are to our friends, family, pets, garden etc. Jane taught me that apologizing to children was a valid and valuable skill, one that I had not understood. Much as in the same way my flatmate (house share friend) many years ago taught me to respect people in customer service and to not take my frustrations out on them when a service was problematic.

So, today I think I learnt, apologizing to yourself has a place. That it is kind to be gentle when things are out of your control, when you don't know what to do. It isn't necessary to be self-critical and expect perfection, or even expect yourself to know what to do. Together people are stronger than alone. Together does not mean partners or spouses, it means people who have formed social or emotional connections that are respectful, caring and kind.

Reach out to your together people when you need and when they might need. Thank you to everyone who is a part of my together, including those who are no longer with us. Arohanui Mike, Grace, Granny G, Granny and Grandad and Jane.

~ 32 ~

ANXIOUS

Inspired by Dr Jane

Jane had a level of anxiety about how others perceived or judged her. She didn't look like a medical doctor with her Celtic and Japanese tattoos visible if she wore short sleeves. In younger doctors this might be more typical, but she was 55 when she died. She worried people thought she wasn't skilled because of her ADHD, when the reality was her patients all loved her and were so grateful for her diagnostic skills and her encyclopedic knowledge of medications.

Termite mounds under the moon
E.Goodall (2018)

I understood her anxiety. When I first got my autism diagnosis, I was worried that people would judge me negatively. Time between diagnosis and PhD was about 6 months. I learnt that people who judge me were not people I needed to worry about. Jane didn't learn this. She was sensitive and cared what people thought.

Jane's GP told her to quit a job that Jane had recently started, remarking that it was a waste of Jane's talents. Sadly, all the years of schoolteachers telling her she wouldn't amount to anything stayed etched in her brain, writ large. Even though she had 'made it', she could hear their negativity whenever someone made a snide comment or was just plain mean or judgemental.

I don't understand why people are mean or judgemental. We can never know someone's story, their why, if we judge them. When we are mean, we cause pain. Why, what for? When things were hard, Jane would be anxious about being anxious. As long as she could look after others, care take, help, she would be ok. If she couldn't the anxiety would build and build.

If I had our time over, I would have adopted a granny for her, to give her someone to look after day in and day out. I think this would have sustained her and kept her anxiety at bay. But mostly, I wish that she had had teachers who cared about her, who noticed her ADHD instead of labelling her as useless and work avoidant.

Jane's work ethic was ridiculous. She worked a full day on the day she died. She worked full-time for the first four years of medical school. She worked two and three jobs for most of the 14 years we were together. She worked more in her short life that I am likely to do in the whole of mine, even if I live another 40 years.

~ 33 ~

BOXES & FILING CABINETS

As a child, I thought everyone organised their memories in a series of boxes and filing cabinets. Some of the boxes have loosely closed lids that could be easily opened, so the contents could be revisited easily and frequently. The equivalent filing cabinet drawers roll in and out smoothly, with paper beautifully ordered in crisp dividers. Other boxes were locked tight and hidden in the dusty crevices of my mind. These were to be ignored totally, in ways that rendered the memories obsolete, erasing them from the timeline of life.

Filing Cabinet
E.Goodall (2020)

The boxes and cabinets are not date ordered, they are grouped either by event or sentinel aspect of; so there is a pencil filing cabinet with memories and stories in which pencils were a key factor. There are lots of food cabinets; places are related to food often, exact meals from 40 years ago preserved intact, with the reason for the memory being little to do with the food. More it is an easy classification system.

I am a super star of organising the boxes and filing cabinets in my brain. It baffles me when people ask me to open one that is deliberately locked. What is the point in shining light on pain or trauma? Is it really true that one can only heal through analysis, or is it true that for some people locking the box and throwing away the key is just as helpful, if not more so? I had to stop the grief counselling that I took up, all it did was try and open my locked box of loss, whilst ignoring my open filing cabinet of gratitude for what came before the loss.

Other people, apparently do not have this beautiful storage system in their minds. I can understand that without it, things need to be dealt with differently, and that this difference is important in the healing process for some. Instead, I have an open box, that sits in my heart, filled with gratitude for all those whanau, family and friends who are walking the journey of my life with me. Whether in short bursts, leaving when their part is needed no more, or longer term. Longer term – holding hands, wiping tears, sharing belly laughs, talking, listening, hearing, never judging, just accepting and loving.

Aroha is undervalued in our world. Without love we are all poorer. I may have lost my loved wife, but I still have so much love in my life, from the fluppy puppy to my Kiwi whanau to my first genuine life mentor/friend. Teaching, guiding, mentoring that are based in love – not sex, love, build solid ground to explore life, learn from mistakes and experience both joys and sorrow. Sorrow held collectively in love is not able to ruin the neat boxes and filing cabinets. Some sorrows are opened and fondly looked over, whilst others are consigned to that black hole of not needed ever again.

Hold your loved ones tightly when they need, and gently when that tight embrace is too painful. Send out the love, through kindness and compassion, to those you meet in the street, at work, in the shops or online.

For those of us with boxes, this keeps our storage rooms in order. For those without, it keeps them grounded in hope.
Arohanui to everyone who has led me to where I am now.

~ 34 ~

LOVE

Inspired by Dr Jane

Jane and I on our wedding day
Lisa Hertling OUAT Wedding Photography 2018

"You cannot love too much or love too many people" Jane said to me when we had just started dating. This was not something I understood at the time. Over the years we were together, I came to embrace her concept of love as a bottomless pool that could give continuously.

Jane had this huge capacity to love, to open her heart and our home to those in need of love and care. She taught me how to share time and resources more generously that I had ever done.

I believe when you love someone you set them free to do what they need to do. Jane wanted to get married to me, so we did. It was a beautiful, special day, shared with family, whanau and friends. The venue staff said it was the best wedding they had ever hosted. There was so much love in the air, you could feel it. We had a child throwing lego during the speeches, chairs on the dance floor so people could sit and dance and at least half the guests are autistic and half are Kiwis. It was relaxed and people could be their authentic selves, lego and all.

I look at our wedding photos and I can see the love between us, but also for us from our guests. I can also see how physically unwell Jane was at the time, and I am glad we got married, that I gave her this gift of love till death do us part. That she knew she was truly loved, valued and valuable, cherished and nurtured. I am glad our son was the ring bearer, that my pounamu became our oathing stone and now carries our wedding vows within.

I am glad I designed our rings and that I now wear hers, with its 'silver fern' and koru made of gold from our family rings and a gold nugget from somewhere she had worked in Australia, symbols that linked our heart home of New Zealand/Aotearoa and our physical home of Australia and linked our lives and spirits together.

I am glad that I loved freely even in the times when it was hard. I am glad that Jane and I loved each other for who we were at each moment in time, even when it was hard. But mostly, I am proud of myself for deciding when Jane got really sick the year before she died, and we thought she might die, that this was not about me, it was about Jane and my job was to love her and support her in her decisions going forward.

When Jane chose to work even though it made her evenings difficult and meant I needed to be her carer as well as her wife. I supported that decision, even though I did not like it, I loved her and that was right for her.

~ 35 ~

LOVE & KINDNESS

Branch full of blossom, SA.
E.Goodall (2020)

This week I have been wondering if love and kindness are one and the same, and it is merely a semantic error that we separate them out in English English. In many languages and cultures, the word that translates to the concept of love is far more encompassing that the English English word love.

This word has three main 'meanings' – platonic (non-sexual) love for your children and extended family members, (sexual) love for you spouse/partner and then a sort of generic 'like a lot' in relation to activities, things, places etc. And yet, strong friendships have a solid foundation of love, which is neither based on family ties, nor on sexual attraction.

A number of years ago, I was privileged to go to the Chatham Islands and in my very basic Te Reo Maori had a conversation with one of the school principals about how aroha (roughly translates as love) needs to underpin quality, effective education. This is not a conversation that could be had in English English. And yet, do we not want out schools to be filled with kindness, compassion and nurturing? A place where each child's spirit is gently held and connected with those of the elders and the educators?

I love my whanau (roughly translates as family) very deeply, in ways that go beyond the English English version of love. My whanau are not related to me and yet I am connected with them, with threads of kindness, value, respect, compassion, safety, security, and aroha.

"Aroha is often translated as "Love", but the full meaning of the word encompasses all of the five senses, the ego and also intellect, and cannot be contained in just one word. In Maori, aroha encompasses the breath of life and the creative force of the spirit, and it assumes that the universe is abundant and that there are more opportunities than people. It seeks and draws out the best in people, it rejects greed, aggression and ignorance and instead encourages actions that are generous." (https://www.neonataltrust.org.nz/2013/11/01/true-meaning-aroha)

I feel that is is this, aroha, that has nurtured and sustained me since my wife died. People who have been generous in their interactions with me, sought to help me reconnect to my creativity and the breath of life within me that was lying quietly, not sure how to move once again.

At times it is like being a teenager, exploring what the world truly means, as I navigate for and by myself, without Jane to translate things that I find baffling. I am naturally shy and contained, but as the kindness in my life continues to build, I find myself less contained and less emotionally isolated. Admittedly, it takes the kindness of others to get me to leave the house, with even Chico playing his part, gently batting me with his paw if I haven't taken him for a walk by 5pm.

I am slowly coming alive again, pretty much all through the kindness of others. I cannot see this kindness as anything other than love, because without love, the same actions would not be kind, but instead be judgemental or coercive. I think, perhaps that culturally, some of us are afraid of love, afraid of valuing more than the body; the spirit and the breath of life. The majority culture in which I live, values materialistic things, things you can touch and see. You cannot see the spirit, but you can certainly touch the spirits of yourself and others, just not physically.

When a friend, family member, colleague or whanau member reaches out and holds my wairua (spirit) gently or safely, I feel alive. I feel valid and valued. Too often we are afraid to reach out in this way, but it gives me great comfort to help others in ways that show value and ensure they feel heard, valid and cared about. But sometimes, great kindness sparks tears in my heart. A wave of sadness washes through me, taking away some of the grief and loss that have built up again. As the wave subsides, so too do the grief and loss.

In your interactions with others this week, take a moment to think about how you behave. Do your words and actions safely hold others or not? Do you bring kindness or could you? I am certainly kinder than I used to be, and some of that immense love that Jane had for so many people seems to have seeped into my psyche, and I am more loving to more people, gentler and kinder.

~ 36 ~

USING HUMOUR TO BE KIND

Inspired by Dr Jane

Jane believed in laughing with people. She was not a typical GP or a typical psychiatric doctor. She would ask people how much weed they smoked, rather than if they smoked, but only when she was sure they did. She used humour to connect and to be kind, to show people that she wasn't looking down on them, that she believed they were her equal.

Jane making me laugh whilst our son took a photo of us at Glenelg, SA.
S.McIlraith (2020)

Jane would say that without people having complex physical and/or complex mental health issues, she wouldn't have a job. This meant that their difficulties paid her wages and so were to be respected. She would say things that other nurses and doctors found outrageous, but that her patients and their families loved, because it marked her as human not someone playing god.

Jane poked fun at herself to both create a bond, but also to lighten her attitude to herself. When we met and I would tell her how intelligent she was, Jane initially refused to believe me, holding on to those childhood memories of being put down in school. I had such different school experiences, being gifted with academic skills and a near perfect auditory memory. I coasted through school with little effort to get near perfect marks (until I didn't but that is another story).

She loved weird and wonderful facts, like whales having menopause and using intergenerational 'parenting' to raise the calves. Her medical error presentations invariably had a picture of a cat looking really sick to introduce the dangers of Paracetamol, which is toxic to cats and can cause major issues when overused in humans.

Jane worked very hard to get her degrees, much harder than I worked, and much harder than many of her peers. She struggled to read due to her very significant ADHD which was both attention deficit and hyperactivity related. Reading requires focus. The funniest moment between us in relation to reading was when she arrived home with a large book on Acceptance and Commitment Therapy that she needed to read and complete the activities it contained as part of her psychiatry training. Jane handed me the book saying; "just give me the summary." She moved into GP training not long after that, missing her stethoscope and unable to sit comfortably practising medicine in a fragmented sense. Jane needed to take a holistic measure of her patients and to work with them to create holistic plans that would maximise quality of life.

Jane had the most infectious smile, and when she laughed her face would light up. I'm not surprised her patients enjoyed spending time with her. They probably felt wrapped in care, in a small sense of the way I did.

~ 37 ~

WINDOWS & DOORS

Sketch of windows and doors
E.Goodall (2020) artist & photographer

You can see through some people's windows, and occasionally through an open door, left open to ease the passage of fresh air through the home. Other doors are firmly shut and we have no idea what goes on behind them, with window coverings that let in light but maintain privacy. A strict barrier between the personal and the other.

As a young teacher, I used to keep my door closed and like many teachers in that era, how I taught behind my classroom door was very different to how I taught when the Principal was walking through. As I have grown older, and vaguely wiser, I have come to understand that what you see through those doors and windows may be pure mirage. When my door is open, what you see is what you get. I am extremely private in many areas of my life, but the rest is an open book.

Like many autistics, I struggle to know when I am looking at a mirage of someone's life and intentions versus the reality. When I get it wrong, it can be devastating. I genuinely don't understand why people would present something that is not an authentic reflection of their true self. Perhaps this is because I am not judgemental on the whole. If you tell me that you take drugs, I am more likely to ask how you find the coming down versus the high, than to judge. But if you tell me that you don't take drugs and then I see you high as a kite, I am bewildered. What does your lie say about you? About me? About the relationship that we have together?

I understand the curtains and steel security bars on the windows and doors to people's innermost secrets, but I can't comprehend painting an elaborate trompe l'oeil to cover up part of your authentic journey. All our journeys' involve difficult choices and wrong paths. It is how we respond to those that matters, not how we pretend they didn't happen. On the other hand, I do not believe I have the right to share the stories from someone else's life journey, unless they have specifically given me consent to do so. Through the generosity of many, I have been able to share stories within my writing, to help others in their journeys. I started writing a book that I working titled, 'The fall out of the dumb stuff I have done, so you don't need to'. I stopped writing it because I realised I wasn't ready to fully open those windows into my life.

It is interesting what we hide behind closed doors. When I worked in crisis support in education, I was always dumbfounded when educators would rule out domestic violence because 'they come from such a nice family.' As a young adult, in one of my first serious relationships, I found out that middle class people just hit where the bruises don't show. A line I repeatedly horrified educators with, without telling them where this knowledge came from. Sadly, I was right more often than they were.

For the last year of Jane's life, our closed doors hid how unwell she was. How much care and support I provided to enable her to work, eat, sleep and be dressed professionally. This was her choice, and her story at the time. Her death made it my story, as my authentic journey shifted from wife and carer to widow. Both of which, carer and widow, erase who you are as an individual, and present words that people use to paint their own mirage. I ceased to exist outside of my work environments as people responded to their mirage and not to me.

This blog was part of my need to exist, to be seen and heard. To make sense of this part of my life journey. At the same time, I have been seeing the elaborate lengths some people go to, to present themselves as something they are not. I present some of me, other bits are still locked in my boxes and filing cabinets, private to not just others, but to me too. I miss Jane's help to translate these false presentations, to explain the emotions behind why people do what they do. I can't help but think, if all the world were autistic, life would be so much easier. We would all say what we meant, and mean what we say. Social justice would be front and centre, and I would hope kindness would be the bedrock.

For me, shame is an unhelpful emotion; it eats up at people and is incompatible with kindness. If we make wrong choices, there is no point in being ashamed. Instead, if we can, we need to make amends, make it right. I am working on this, even when the wrong choice was only wrong because the door looked open and when I walked through the door, I broke it. I am not ashamed of this, it was a genuine mistake, but I do want to make it right, and I am genuinely upset that someone else was hurt by this.

When you are interacting with others, please think about how the way you tweak your truths impacts others around you. Will you accidentally hurt someone? Will your relationships develop small cracks that slowly drive you apart, or will they implode leaving one or more of you devastated? Because a small tweak, a mirage, a tromp l'oiel, they are all just lies. And when we lie, it is not that lie that is the biggest problem, it is the implication that everything that has been said or left unsaid, is a lie, that there is no relationship foundation, just a quicksand of maybes.

Jane was obsessed with being truthful, in herself, in her work, in her relationships. She needed those she loved to be honest with her. I will leave you today with her truth for the last year, in relation to her health, and my final understanding of what she meant.

Jane: *"Time will either heal or reveal."*

My final understanding 'reveal meant death'. We both knew, we just drew the curtains.

~ 38 ~

TIME

Jane's time timer
E.Goodall (2020)

Inspired by Dr Jane

Time meant virtually nothing to Jane. Life was meant to be lived with purpose and value, but otherwise time was a construct sent to annoy. An hour initial consult with her could end up taking two to two and a half hours. Jane was thorough in her case history taking and therapeutic relationship building.

Employers despaired of her being able to make them money and I encouraged her to set up on her own. People she knew, who didn't understand encouraged her to work faster, make more money. But money, like time was unimportant. Making that positive difference was all that ever mattered. If it took fifteen minutes, all good, but if it took a series of hour or two visits, that was all good too.

The only time that time was problematic was when Jane was a patient in hospital herself. She hated every minute, desperately wanting to be home. The time dragged slowly. No matter how much I visited.

I need to be on time, so much so that I have had to stop wearing a watch. Jane could turn up to watch a movie after it started, because it was the experience that was important and because she would have got distracted by something on the way. It was hard to be angry with someone who is late because they were 'saving lives. Although as Jane would say, "doctors don't save lives, vaccines do", which was ironic as she did literally save the lives of a number of people over the years. Including a mother and her unborn baby, a friend of hers and a local who was planning to go fishing offshore, which would have ended his life.

She would wonder, if she took less time with people, would their lives have lasted as long or have been as high quality?

I got her a time timer (shown in the photo) to help her try and get some sense of time. The idea being that after an hour of paperwork, she would have a break, eat or sleep etc. I'd love to say it helped, but it didn't. Jane was always surprised when the alarm rang, that an hour had already passed. She really had no sense of time, her internal body clock not in sync with the construct of time as experienced by many majority culture individuals in Australia and New Zealand.

~ 39 ~

FRIENDS

Sunset at Moana Beach, SA
E.Goodall (2020)

I have the most amazing, non-judgemental, kind and caring friends. Jane's birthday was about 3 weeks ago, and I have been slowly spirally out of emotional control since then. But not noticing it. Sometimes, my incredible lack of insight is astounding.

I knew something was wrong when I was on the loud AC/DC for days rather than one album. When I shouted f*&% on repeat for three days, including whilst watching the sun set over the beach (photo above). And when I made some really dumb decisions. Friends said; 'be kind to yourself, it's ok to make mistakes', 'what can I do to help?', 'I've booked lunch, see you there' and 'I wish I was there to give you a big hug.'

Then I realised I was angry, really really angry, about Jane being dead, about me having to wait at least a year to find out why she died, even though the coroner has the results from her autopsy and further investigations. About not being able to take her ashes home, because of covid. About not being able to see my son, our whanau, have my feet on the land that calls my heart and wairua. About being in pain that I don't want to be in.

Friends and neighbours have checked in with me and listened kindly, sharing their experiences of grief and pain. Letting me know, the journey is hard and that it is normal for pain to rear its head and swipe you off the path forward when you least expect it. I get irrationally angry at memes that suggest we should be strong and bounce back when life is hard. I want to hide away and cocoon myself in the vague hope the pain and anger will go away.

Friends have gently but firmly pointed out, my penchant for boxes and filing cabinets does not mean I can actually put my grief, loss and pain into a box, lock it and have it stay locked. Their gentleness reassures me that though I lost my wife, my love, that I am still loved and cared about. Their kindness in continually reminding me to be compassionate to myself, in the same way that I am to others is helpful. It really is ok, to not be ok.

I never realised how many friends I do have. How many people genuinely like me and care about me. Until recently, when Jane persuaded me to change my attitude, my default position was that anyone I met, disliked me. This was mainly a protective mechanism – people can't hurt you as much if you don't let them get close. It doesn't matter if people don't like you if you already assigned that role to them. Jane's big heart hurt for me when I would say that people didn't like me. Although to be fair, even she agreed that some people really don't like me!

What is interesting is that, I have always tried to be kind to people, whether or not I classify them as a friend. Kindness and friendship are not the same, though the latter requires the former. And yet, I have not expected kindness from others, nor always extended it to myself. Why is it, that we, as people, do this? This week when people have asked me how I am, I have answered truthfully. Not one person has responded with anything other than kindness. I am ever grateful that I work with people who genuinely care about each other and that I am surrounded by people who remind me that I am not walking this journey by myself, even when it is incredibly hard.

Please keep asking those around you if they are ok, but also ask them to share a meal with you or go for a walk or drive with you, or if your lockdown means none of these are possible; to share a late night text chat full of honesty, raw emotions and deep meaning. All of these have been invaluable in getting me through this week.

I did have some good news this week. The lump that I found in my breast, is not breast cancer. The mammogram was painful but not too bad, the ultrasound took an hour and then the additional mammogram, to check the initial 'not good' finding was excruciating and I nearly passed out. The specialist had explained they needed to squash just the area with the 'lines on the first mammogram' to see 'if the lines go away' and if so then it was all good and if not, they would need to think what to do next. So they squashed about 3cms wide, and squashed and squashed. I forgot to breathe, because it hurt so much. It was over in about 10 seconds, then the technician left to talk with the specialist. And then I got the all clear and got to go home and breathe. It was the only moment all week that I wasn't angry or anxious or sad. I was relieved.

Which made me angry. Because relief was one of the early grief emotions for me. Jane had been so unwell, she had suffered so much, that her painless and instant death was a relief in some ways. She was no longer suffering, and in turn, I was no longer watching her suffer, which is a particular kind of torture that I would not wish on anyone, ever. Be nice to those you love, life is short, no matter how long it lasts. Arohanui.

~ 40 ~

PEOPLE

Inspired by Dr Jane

Jane people watching before she got sick.
E.Goodall (2015)

"I just love people watching," Jane would say as she sat facing others when we were out. And she did, she was truly fascinated by people, and understood them in ways that I, her autistic wife, did not. Although, she too either trusted too much or not enough.

When we first were dating and I met her whanau and best friends, they warned me. If I hurt her, they would hunt me down and make me pay. As I lived around the corner from them, and I interpret language literally, this was quite a threat. They are now as firmly embedded in my heart as they were in hers.

With a few exceptions (*'Frizzie'* who treated her unfairly, and her teachers who had been mean to her), Jane loved people. She wanted to share her successes with others and bring them along with her. She truly felt that what was hers (or mine) was for those who needed it more than us. People's motivations intrigued her, and I truly miss her helpful explanations for things that continue to baffle me.

Jane would announce that she had invited friends or whanau to stay with us for a few weeks, filled with joy. And I, I would fret. Noise, lack of privacy and peace. But, and it is such a big but, Jane was right. We need people, we need positive, trusting, loving interactions with people. It is good and right to share our successes. Material wealth hoarded is misery, material wealth shared in ways that ease suffering, create opportunities, is a joy for all involved.

There is good in all people. Jane had an interesting skill for seeing the potential in adults, a skill I had only for children and young people when I met her. Over time, I came to see the same things she saw in the adults around her. People all have potential, to be good, to be kind, to make a positive difference. Sometimes they are lost in themselves and sometimes they are lost in the world.

Jane could reach out and metaphorically hold their hand, walk alongside them, if they let her. This is something I can do, I do now. Thinking of how it was natural to Jane, how it is not quite natural for me, but that that is ok. It is still positive and kind, caring and compassionate. Cherish everyone, all the time. If we all did this, the people of this world would suffer so much less.

~ 41 ~

KINDNESS & JOY

Almost broken neurodiverse kiwi
E.Goodall (2020) artist & photographer

Sometimes we find joy in the tiniest things; a flower in the park, the giggle of a child in the street, the snuggle of the dog. But sometimes we need to be kind to ourselves, to say it is ok to have a moment of joy. Not in ways that might hurt others, but in those moments where we subconsciously chose not to do something. When that something may be out of character or atypical for society, we deny ourselves those moments of joy.

I have a stim that really calms me and I used to not do it, because I worried other people might judge me. As a result my tics would get worse and I would feel so much more stressed.

With just a little bit of kindness to myself, I let myself rub my thumb and fingers over each other, slow and fast, gentle and firm. A tiny burst of joy counteracts all the other emotions and calm descends.

I am going to be kinder to myself. It is ok to have moments of joy. To share them. To create them. To gift them to myself or others.

I am not perfect. I am not always kind to myself or others but I do try. But that effort has always been outward focused. This has been a hard week. And several people have told me I need to be kinder to myself. I have heard and they were right.

Thanks. Arohanui to all those struggling at the moment.

~ 42 ~

STRUGGLES

Beach in the Northern Territory
E.Goodall (2018)

Inspired by Dr Jane

Pain and ill-health were a serious struggle in the last years of Jane's life. My younger brother asked my parents if Jane was dying of cancer, because the photos I proudly posted to Facebook of my lovely partner, made him worry. This was a few years before we got married, before she nearly died twice. Once from multiple pulmonary emboli and once from something that left her with a paralysed arm and limited mobility for several months.

Jane decided after that, that she didn't want to go back to hospital again. Ever. That she would rather die than go back. Her DNR (do not resuscitate) was legally documented and I respected her choices. I did try to resuscitate her when I found her dead, my human instinct overriding conscious thought for almost an hour. At that point I asked the ambulance staff to stop, recalling her DNR. They had already had to stop defibrillating anyway, knowing they could not bring her back but wanting to let me know they were doing everything possible.

Jane struggled with daily pain, with all the other things that went along with whatever it was that was causing her body to stop functioning when she was tired or overwhelmed. She struggled with how much independence it stole, with the possibility that she would have to stop work. Jane wanted to work to the very end, and she did.

Jane struggled with how people treated me when they knew I was autistic, and it prevented her from being more open about her ADHD. She struggled with internalised homophobia for many years, but left that behind when we got married. A day that brought her and I, and our friends, family and whanau, so much joy. Jane struggled with learning difficulties that had never been recognised when she was at school, and made her university studies hard. But she had perseverance in unlimited quantities. What she wanted, she worked at until she got. Her work ethic meaning that she would just work and work and work until it all paid off.

I am not sure that Jane ever knew how many people liked her, nor how many loved her. She struggled in a very different way to me in relation to how we saw other people and how we thought they saw us. She felt invisible most of the time and dismissed much of the time. Not at home, at home, she felt safe and many of the struggles fell away. She loved my company and enjoyed spending time with my parents. Other than that, she struggled with culture shock, Australia being significantly different than 'back home', New Zealand. When home, in New Zealand, Jane was so much more relaxed, even when she was so unwell on our last visit. Planned to say goodbye, in case she didn't make it. She didn't.

~ 43 ~

FOLDED ROCKS

Uluru, NT.
E.Goodall (2020)

One of the things I love to do it take photos out of windows, car windows, plane windows, building windows. As you pass over or through the outback in the Northern Territory, the landscape has powerful markers of water, wind, sand and stone. Folded rocks mark the passage of time since the earth was young.

I think my heart has folded, marking the sentinel events in my life, like the folded rocks record geological highlights. As we age, the folds of life are written not just on our faces, but also in our hearts. Neither good, nor bad, these folds keep secrets tucked out of sight and love anchored.

~ 44 ~

SECRETS

Rain clouds over Moana Beach
E.Goodall (2020)

Inspired by Dr Jane

"It's lying by omission. You know I don't tolerate lies."

Jane didn't believe in secrets, she would buy me a birthday present and then excitedly tell me all about it, months before my birthday. This doesn't mean she didn't have secrets tucked out of sight.

A fiancé that had died in an accident before they could get married. I still do not know the whole story.

At the end of her life, Jane wanted to keep a bigger secret. How sick she was. She didn't want pity, and she hated being fussed over. It was hard enough for her, that I knew, and I cared for and about her. Only a handful of people knew how worried I was that she was dying. Even then, I kept her secrets about why I thought this. I will respect her privacy, which was so important to her.

We prepared our house for her, in case she needed to use a wheelchair. Friends of friends and tradies fitted our accessibility conversion into their busy schedules, and it meant I could keep working as she could sit in the shower. Without it, I couldn't leave the house in case she insisted on having a shower and then collapsed. Her fierce determination could not override her failing body, no matter how much she thought it could.

~ 45 ~

MILESTONES

Sunset at Kata Tjuta, NT
E.Goodall (2020)

Next week it is our son's birthday. Jane always did the birthday thing, the presents the cards. Although she would inevitably forget to write or send the card, presents usually made it before or on time. I found a collection of cards she had bought for me over the years, carefully selected cards to convey exactly what she wanted to say to me, her wife, on birthdays, Christmas etc. Mostly unwritten, stored in her bedside drawers ready to be passed over if her attention was caught at the right moment.

Our son won't mind if he doesn't have a present or a card, which is good as with the snail speed of hard copy mail these days, a card would arrive a month late. I haven't done anything with Jane's card collection. It is one of the too hard basket tasks.

Another one is a form that I need to do before probate can get filed. I just can't do it. I know I need to, and I have set a deadline of before our son's birthday. His first birthday without her, one of his mum's. And I cannot be there. My heart hurts for this milestone.

I had assumed on her first 'not alive anymore' birthday that I would be fine. I wasn't. I hope our son is ok. My love can hold him tight, but I cannot hug him across cyber space. I can tell him how proud Jane was of him, but I cannot walk on the beach with him. Our words carried by the wind as our toes dig into the sand and the waves crash nearby.

I am 50 next year. Jane had all these plans to celebrate. I am not big on celebrating milestones. Mainly because I worry no-one will want to turn up to celebrate with me or that too many people will and it will be overwhelming. In and between that I have/had an academic achievement to celebrate (I made myself nice food and started to make a dress), our sons birthday (I will phone him), our wedding anniversary (I have no idea how to get through that one), Christmas (don't even think about it), New Year (I have a friend who I have celebrated that with before when Jane just wanted to go to bed early as she was tired or unwell, so that is sorted and really I think I have used up all my bad karma, next year has to be better).

It is tempting to ignore all the milestones. To just live moment to moment. To give up on celebrating, but the pull to step into joy momentarily is strong. A beautiful sunset or sunrise gives me so much joy. I laid some of Jane's ashes to rest in the Northern Territory last week. A place that she felt spiritually at home in. It brought me some peace and a dance from a bird, that spend half an hour visiting and showing me it's tail fanned out.

But the heartache that followed was hard. The rest of her ashes need to go home to Aotearoa. I feel the pull but it is not possible yet with all the travel restrictions. I am trying to be comfortable with uncomfortable feelings. To just sit with the pain and then to take Chico for a walk and revel in his joy and he bounds around the park.

Chico loves to dance with me. When I am needing a zoom break, sometimes I put the music on and dance, dog on hip. He loves it and his joy is infectious. For a few minutes I am alive again. Alive rather than exisiting is not a consistent state currently.

When I am connected with someone or something or someplace, then I am alive. Connecting with whanau brings a special reward of non-judgemental acceptance, a beautiful way to be alive. I do not need people to be around me all the time. Connecting does not need to be physical, in real life or in person. But it does need to be and Jane did most of the bridge building that enabled me to connect. I do not know how to explain myself to people who do not get me.

I do not understand people who are judgemental in any way. It turns out there are a lot of them. I get they have a different life journey to me. Sometimes I can explain why they may day or do the things they do, but I can't justify them. But then, I know people do not understand my very autistic sense of social justice and how this does not necessarily match non-autistic views of social justice. That two competing needs may be evaluated quite differently by me than by them.

With colleagues I just delivered a webinar on autism and friendships. I am very grateful to have so many kind and caring friends and I will try not to fixate on the few people that I now know are not friends. That realisation that people you thought of as friends are not friends anymore (or perhaps never were) is one of the suckiest milestones in life. It hurts as much as it did when I was 6 or 16.

I have chosen to ignore being ignored at the moment. Because perhaps I am wrong. There is no socially acceptable way to ask a non-autistic person if they aren't talking to you anymore. I did try, by text. I regret that but I can't undo it. If you grow out of a friendship just let the person know, according to various threads on Reddit, not just autistics are traumatised by being ghosted. People poured out their hearts and hurts about being ghosted decades ago or recently.

I am not hurting on that level as I rationalise that if someone is willing to ghost then they were not a friend in the first place. If I did something wrong or they think I did, which is highly likely, then they should say. Then I could give the explanation which is quite different to the assumption (that I hear on the metaphorical grapevine). But in the end, all anyone can do is live their life as best they can as we can't make people understand us.

~ 46 ~

THE END

Our civil union double koru 'heart'
E.Goodall (2020) photo only

It is the time of year when clocks go forward in some places, back in others and yet stay the same in yet others. New Zealand's clocks went forward this week and ours in South Australia go forward next week. (Spring forward/fall back).

I really struggle to grasp time zones. Intellectually I totally get them but emotionally. Nah. And now I have this weird BJD and AJD time too (before Jane died/after Jane died). The way I measure time has changed. A song can last for a whole 30 minutes (literally as it gets put on repeat over and over) or a few bars can be unbearable to listen to for any longer.

Time stands still when bad news arrives and then does weird things for months and months. I remember sitting on the floor howling when Mike died. I can only have been 20 or so and he was only a year older than me. We had had a tumultuous relationship built on teenage angst and alienation. His emotional pain leaked out of him and when he found someone who could take it away somehow for a few moments he would hold onto them.

I used to spend Sundays with him. Cooking his family their Sunday lunch with him, whilst they were at church. They were the source of his pain. I didn't recognise nor speak to them at the funeral. I know they would have been there. It was held at their church.

Time has been stretched and compressed since Jane died. Some days are slow and painful whilst others have moments of joy that pass too quickly to hold onto. I understand why Mike held onto the people he held onto now. Those moments can only build up into meaningful chunks of time if they repeat enough.

I looked at the weeds in my 'garden' today and thought about how much time had passed since I last weeded. I hate gardening. I love the idea of it. But not the reality. I had actually weeded though and it was looking good, with all Jane's jasmine in flower and the aloe vera happily multiplying. A few months. A few months passed since I weeded. How? What was I doing that I didn't see the weeds start to grow? They are way bigger than the dog, surely I could have walked over and pulled them out at some stage?

The inertia that sits on my shoulders sometimes is not something I am used to. BJD I don't think I would have had more than a few days in my life. Now, clearly I can have months of inertia. I know I am busy doing other things, but not 24/7 busy. I know I have hours of free time because I have been watching hours of tv. I gave back the Foxtel box when I cancelled Jane's account. I couldn't watch tv without her for a few months. Now I watch hours of things she would never have watched. Some of it is so bad I have to turn it off, occasionally it is engaging. I am writing or weaving at the same time. So, I could have walked outside and pulled the weeds out.

Time has always been so important to me, but I think it is less so now. I do not need to be on time to the minute anymore. Because no-one will die if I am a minute late. There are more important things than being on time. Being kind and considerate for one. This may translate as being approximately on time or early. I thought about wearing a watch again for the first time in over a year. Maybe when the clocks change. I am waking up as if they already have changed. Sparkly wide awake at 5:30 or 6, having never woken up at that time unless the alarm was set for then. Usually to get a flight. Now, I just am awake. Wide awake. Ready for the day. Or at least engaged with the day.

Time does not heal. Time plays tricks. Things seem to be getting better then they go back again. Perhaps First People's cyclical concepts of time are more accurate than the Western linear ideas. Perhaps the soft ebb and flow of time has a fierce undercurrent that can override and overwhelm.

None of us know how much time we have. Whether it is time on earth, time with a particular person or in a particular place. Spend your time wisely to minimise regrets and maximise the good in life. Take the time to show those you love how much you appreciate them. And don't waste time on those who detract from your life. It's ok to unfriend people in real life, not just on social media! But before you do, take a few minutes to evaluate the pros and cons. Then move forward.

Arohanui.

~ 47 ~

IDEAS FROM JANE

- Bleach baths (highly diluted) are great
- People who don't love their animals aren't trustworthy
- If you can't trust someone your car, don't let them look after your dog
- Coming home to your dog makes the day better, no matter what
- Make a difference, leave the world a better place than you found it
- Be kind, seek to understand
- Share music
- Don't have regrets, die content (she was more content in the last month than she had ever been)
- Marry the love of your life, work hard at the relationship and stay committed. Marriage is till death 'do us part' (and death did indeed part us)
- Have faith in your kids, your partner, your friends. Help them to believe in themselves and give them a hand up, not a hand out.

~ 48 ~

THINGS TO DO TO PREPARE

1. Get your will drawn up by a lawyer
2. Have a current advanced care directive
3. Make sure if you are a couple that you each have your own bank account, which your salary/benefits get paid into. The banks can freeze the accounts when you die.
4. If you have kids/pets include what is to happen with them in the will if you both die or you are a single parent (kids or fur babies), WITH the agreement of the people who you want to take care of them.
5. Make sure you know each other's 'important details', bank account numbers, superannuation member numbers, where the car ownership papers are insurance details are kept.
6. Be open and talk about what you want to happen after you die. Do you want burying or cremating? Where? What type of service? How much money do you want spending on the service etc?
7. Know who needs to be notified and have a plan how to. Know how to change the voicemail of the person who died, and how to put an autoreply on all their email accounts. To do this you will need to know their logins. Keep them in a safe place.

~ 49 ~

THE INSPIRATION & THE AUTHOR

Dr Jane and Dr Emma (Wedding Day)

Dr Jane Nugent Wife, GP, Noctor (Nurse/Doctor) An inspiration 8/8/1964-18/4/2020	Dr Emma Goodall Author (Me) Photographer, painter, sculptor, researcher

Dr Emma Goodall is an autistic author, researcher and consultant. She works full time in the field of autism and also runs a consultancy, Healthy Possibilities, that focuses on interoception, life coaching and education.

Dr Jane Nugent was a nurse first and then a Medical Doctor with a special interest and additional qualifications in psychopharmacology and General Practice. Dr Nugent lectured across Australia and New Zealand in pathophysiology, medical errors and pharmacology, she believed medicine was an art that needed to take into account the whole person. Jane left school very young and went from being a cleaner to a doctor - the long route to medicine. She was my partner for 14 years, civil unioned for 10 before we married. Jane died less than 18 months after we got married.

Jane left behind me, her wife, our son, her two brothers, her whanau - Michelle, Duane and the kids, my parents as well as her patients, colleagues and friends. She was well loved and respected for her big heart and her encyclopedic knowledge of drugs and medical issues.

www.ingramcontent.com/pod-product-compliance
Ingram Content Group UK Ltd.
Pitfield, Milton Keynes, MK11 3LW, UK
UKHW021254180426
11947UKWH00010B/768